Celtic Treasury
The Art and History of the Celts
CATRIONA LUKE

'Carpet' page of the Lichfield Gospels, folio 220, c. 720. Bird interlace, which owed its form to Germanic art, but its subject to Celtic, had been perfected at the Lindisfarne scriptorium. Here it is at its most complex and ambitious and on an angular Saxon cross which reflects the different influences of the south of Britain. The gospels were probably inscribed in Mercia in the early eighth century.

LICHFIELD CATHEDRAL

Celtic Treasury
the art and history of the celts
CATRIONA LUKE

Opening page of the Christmas Gospel of St Matthew, folio 11, Echternach Gospels, c. 700. The gospel begins with the traditional Greek abbreviation for Christ, XPI from ΧΡΙΣΤΟΣ, but is less ornate than that of Kells. The liberal use of gold ink was a continental influence.

BIBLIOTTEKET KUNGL, STOCKHOLM

PAST TIMES™
Oxford, England

Special Edition for PAST TIMES™, Oxford, England

First published in Great Britain in 1996 by Michael O'Mara Books
9 Lion Yard, Tremadoc Road, London SW4 7NQ

A CIP catalogue record for this book is available from the British Library

ISBN 1–85479–723–9

10 9 8 7 6 5 4 3 2 1

Typeset by Keystroke, Jacaranda Lodge, Wolverhampton
Printed and bound in Spain by Artes Graficas Toledo S.A.
D.L.TO: 564-1996

Book design by David Fordham
PICTURE ACKNOWLEDGMENTS
All pictures, except for those on p6,11, kindly supplied by The Bridgeman Art Library
p11 British Museum, London. p6 National Museum of Ireland.

CONTENTS

THE ART OF THE EARLY CELTS

O F ALL THE PEOPLE WHO INHABITED ANCIENT AND EARLY MODERN EUROPE, some of the most remarkable and distinctive were the Celts. Over a period of two and a half thousand years, from 1,600 BC to AD 850, their artistic culture survived intact, with the particular Celtic voice and style largely unaltered. The Celts were skilled and sophisticated craftsmen who worked precious metals and stones with the same assurance as the artists and metalworkers of the great ancient civilizations of Egypt, Assyria, Greece and Rome, but because they were neither builders, administrators, nor men of letters, lasting edifices in stone or written literature do not survive. Instead, they remain for us elusive, half-glimpsed amongst their tombs, jewellery, weaponry, fantastical myths and legends, and in the early medieval Christian manuscripts which were their finest achievements.

Ireland's goldwork from the mid-Bronze Age. There were two periods where gold was plentiful in Ireland and Britain; one from 2,100–1,600 BC, the other from the later Iron Age c. first century BC. This neckring, sometimes called a lunular, reflects the sun cult at the centre of Celtic beliefs.

Theirs was an abstract art, the origin of which lay in the choice and combination of motifs, mainly from the world of nature, with only occasional human elements. It is the art of people intensely and fully aware of their environment and of the permanent presence of a mirrored Otherworld, unseen, which informed their spirituality. The natural and the spiritual combined to form the thread that runs through their work, from the early sun-shaped torques of the second millennium BC to the meticulous tapestry of triskeles and interlace, animals, and birds that appear in the gospels of Lindisfarne, Durrow and Kells.

While they created a form of line and space which was very much their own, the Celts were great borrowers of motifs, precious materials and forms from other cultures. Their achievement was to free classical motifs, making them supple and flowing, and extending their design potential. The friezes, palmettes and lotus flowers of Greek and Oriental art became bound into the artists' vocabulary, but refined and simplified into flowing lines. To an instinctive sense of composition they brought an intellectual discipline. Elaborate compass work produced designs of mathematical proportion, which none the less were mesmerically flowing and curvilinear in production.

Celtic art could only have maintained its continuity of form and treatment because it satisfied, over a long period of time, a way of seeing. It was a religious art and its symbolism and abstraction denoted a complex and highly developed system of religious beliefs. The Celts perceived in all aspects of the natural world – each tree, river, spring, lake and mountain – the presence of spirits which were alive in a supernatural way. Trees represented fertility, rebirth and the sacred link between the earth, the sky and the Underworld; wheels and circles symbolized the sun, the sky god and thunder. Fire, an important part of ceremonies held three times a year in May, August and November, was the great cleanser and from its ashes sprang new life. Water was worshipped as creator and destroyer and all sources of water, including the spirit-filled marshes, were sacred. (The ritual depositing of weaponry in sacred lakes and rivers is a consistent feature of Celtic religious practice throughout Europe. Bent weapons were cast into the lake of Lyn Cerrig Bach on Anglesey in the first century AD and it is not difficult to see the parallels with Arthurian legend: Sir Thomas Malory tells us in *Le Morte D'Arthur* that Arthur, on the point of death, instructed Sir Bedivere: 'Take thou Excalibur, my good sword, and go with it to yonder water side, and when thou comest there I charge thee throw my sword in that water.') Lakes and rivers were concerned with passage into the Otherworld, springs were associated with healing, and wells were revered for their physical link with the Underworld and for the wisdom that reputedly lay at the bottom of them. Numbers too were mystical. Triple was deemed to be the natural order of things, so sky, earth and Underworld went together; earth, air and water; past, present and future. Celtic society itself was organized in the tripartite hierarchy of kings, a warrior nobility and farmers, the druids being drawn from the second class.

At the heart of the Celtic panoply of gods and goddesses, of which it is estimated there were four hundred – sixty-nine of them devoted to war alone – was the sun, the mother goddess, provider of abundance and life. Some of the earliest goldwork of the Celts are the lunulas, or gold collars, of Ireland, which are themselves engraved with simple circles, undoubtedly sun motifs. From the mid-Bronze Age, and probably from much earlier, the image of the sun appears in the form of a spoked wheel. Warriors wore amulets with solar motifs as protection in battle, and people were buried with these amulets and accompanied by miniature sun symbols to ease their journey to the Otherworld. Little figurines made of clay, found in central Gaul and Brittany, have solar symbols on their bodies and perhaps performed the same function. In Ireland, the goddess Eriu bore the golden cup full of red liquor which was handed to mortal kings as a legitimization of their kingship. Horses were also linked to the solar cult, considered, as in so many Indo-European cults, to be divine creatures since they pulled the chariot that carried the sun across the sky.

In contrast to the mysticality of their religious beliefs, we know from contemporary sources and from the content of their legends and romances that the Celts were an ebullient, high-spirited people, fond of ornament and bright clothes, gambling, hunting and intellectual pursuits. They were feasters and drinkers; war-mongers – by Roman accounts 'madly fond of war' – who were also known for their hospitality; adventurers, seafarers and traders. They were fearless and brutal fighters who took their enemies' heads in battle, but they also loved poetry and song, had a streak of whimsy and a fondness for puns and verbal jokes. The Romans thought them 'straightforward and not of evil character', and a rather vain people, who accordingly were 'unbearable in victory' and utterly 'downcast in defeat'. One commentator remarked upon their childish boastfulness and love of decoration: 'They wear ornaments of gold, torques on their necks, and bracelets on their arms and wrists, while people of high rank wear dyed garments besprinkled with gold.'

Celtic society was based on kinship, in which feasting played an important role. The joining of dynastic families, peace treaties, the celebration of victory all demanded ratification by shared food and drink. To the Romans' amazement, 'they invite strangers to their banquets and only after the meal do they ask who they are and of what they are in need.' Such hospitality, endearing though it is, was the softer side of a competitive people.

Polybius reports that at the battle of Telemon in 225 BC, 'all the warriors in the front ranks were adorned with gold necklaces and bracelets.' The accumulation and possession of wealth mattered to kings and nobles almost as much as the need to defend their honour in battle. Torques, or elaborate gold necklaces, were worn throughout the Celtic world and were not just items of jewellery, but also units of wealth, and symbols of high status and even of divine power. They had mystical and religious significance: a torque worn by an antlered god can be seen on the Gundestrop cauldron dating from the second century BC.

> Dio Cassius, the Roman historian, described Queen Boudica as wearing: 'a great twisted golden necklace at her throat'. The great Snettisham torque was found in the royal treasury of the Iceni and is romantically associated with Queen Boudica. It was actually buried a century before she lived, but the style of the Snettisham goldsmiths would have varied little. Torques had great mystical and religious significance in the warrior-dominated society of the Celts.
>
> BRITISH MUSEUM

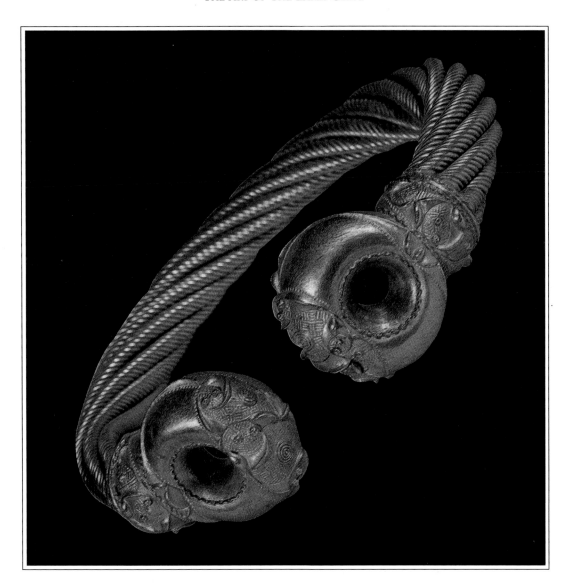

Precious stones, gold and silk were equally admired and provide evidence that the continental Celts had important links with places very far away indeed. A burial chamber at Hochmichele contained fabric from a woman's dress embroidered with original Chinese silk thread. In the area around the rich saltmines of Hallstatt in the sixth century BC, an acquisitive Celtic aristocracy imported ivory from Africa, great quantities of amber from the Baltic and gold from the East. A princely tomb at Hochdorf, which dates from this period, is an Aladdin's cave of ostentatious wealth. The prince was covered from head to toe in gold – shoes, torque, armrings and brooches – and lay in state on a long bronze couch amidst richly embroidered textiles and hangings. There are wonderful incidental possessions: a low cone-shaped hat made of two round discs of birch bark stitched together; a large iron razor and nail scissors; and nine drinking horns.

HE DISTANT ORIGINS OF THE CELTS ARE UNCERTAIN. THEY were nomadic people, hunter-gatherers, whose numerous tribes occupied much of Europe and particularly northern and central Europe between 2,000 and 100 BC, the peak of their influence being *c.* 500–100 BC when their territory extended from Ireland in the west, across central and eastern Europe to Galatia in Asia Minor (present-day Turkey). The Greeks called them *keltoi* and it is from their chronicles that nineteenth-century historians dated the emergence of the Celts to the sixth century BC. Xenophon mentions them as mercenaries against the Thebans in the Peloponnesus in 369 BC and Plato includes them in a list of barbarian people prone to drunkenness.

In the present century the timescale has broadened. Analysis of the modern Celtic languages (Irish Gaelic, Welsh, Cornish and Breton), study of early medieval Irish law and literature, carbon dating and proper cataloguing of art and artefacts have greatly increased our knowledge of Celtic history. What has emerged is a picture of a slow but consistent westward movement of an Indo-European people who arrived in waves from eastern Europe and central Asia, from around 2,500 BC.

An early characteristic of these people was the method they used to bury their warriors. From the fourteenth century BC there was a culture in central Europe and as far west as Catalonia and Valencia, distinguished by the custom of burying their dead in burial chambers in mounds called *tumuli*. Their weapons were decorated in particular and distinctive ways, and their language is echoed in modern place names: *briga* (hill), *magus* (plain), *dunum* (fort) passed into Irish (*bri* – hill, *mag* – plain) and Welsh (*bre* – hill). The name of the Rhine is thought to be Celtic, and those of the Nekar, Ruhr and Lippe too.

Since Celtic is an Indo-European language, a cousin of Sanskrit and ancient Greek, Asiatic roots were looked for. In 1908 fragments of manuscripts were found in East Turkestan which were closely linked to Celtic and Italic (Italic being a precursor to Latin). Clay tablets were also found at Boghazkoi in Asia Minor bearing the Hittite language with a special affinity to the two languages. Celtic is linked to Italic from about 2,000 BC, and Italo-Celti, an archaic language of the Indo-European family, seems to have been a distinct group of dialects, different from Greek and Germanic, spoken north of the Alps from around 2,000 BC. Most remarkable of all, Old Irish in its grammar and syntax and even in some vocabulary resembles Sanskrit and the dialects of Central Asia. In poetic metre, there are still traces of Indo-European cadence in Old Irish verse.

Echoes of mid-Asiatic origin persist in rites of kingship, kinship and early laws, and in myths and legends. The Celtic druids, who had complex roles as learned men, priests, genealogists and lawyers, were guardians of an oral tradition which was fundamental to Celtic society and performed for it the same function as the brahmin priests in India. The religious rites of the druids must have remained intact for hundreds, even thousands of years. Caesar, writing in 54 BC about the druids of Gaul noted that they had 'much knowledge of the stars and their motion, of the size of the world and of the earth, of natural philosophy, and the powers and spheres of action of the immortal

gods, which they discuss and hand down to their young students'. The oldest passages of written Irish law tracts, which date from the sixth and seventh century AD, show great similarities with the Hindu Laws of Manu. The four-generational family unit, for example, is identical in Hindu, Irish and Welsh canonical law, so too the law of 'appointed' daughter – a daughter chosen by her father to bear him a grandson if he has no sons and to inherit land – and the eight recognized forms of marriage.

There are elements of Greek, Indian and even Egyptian stories in Celtic myths and many of the motifs are similar: bulls, quests, virility, the search for self, rites of passage. The stories are of warriors, debts and obligations of honour, disguise, beautiful and deceiving women, sacred places – forests, lakes and rivers – and magical animals. Many of the stories hinge on quests for ownership, including the famous Irish tale the Cattle Raid of Cooley.

One of a pair of bronze wine flagons from the Basse-Yutz region of France, fourth century BC. The flagons exhibit many Hallstatt and La Tène motifs. The handle formed out of the arched back of a wolf or dog, the duck bobbing along the spout in anticipation of the river of wine and the chequerboard coral work on the underside of the spout belong to Hallstatt. The four stylized lotus buds on the stopper and the use of palmettes belong to La Tène.
BRITISH MUSEUM

Within their cycles of tales the Celts had their own understanding of their origins. The earliest group of Irish stories, which dates from the Iron Age, is the *Leabhar Gabhála*, or *Book of Invasions*. The myriad Celtic gods and goddesses are explained by the invasion of the *Tuatha Dé Danann*, or divine race from the East, who had to drive out the indigenous *Fomhoire*, or evil spirits of Ireland. The *Tuatha Dé* brought with them four archetypal Indo-European mystical symbols: the Stone of Fál, which cried out at the touch of a rightful king, and which can be seen to this day on the hill of Tara; the Sword of Nuada, from which no-one escaped; the Spear of Lugh, which guaranteed victory; and the Cauldron of Daghda, from which no one departed unsatiated. There were three craft gods: Goibhniu was the Smith God, Luchta the Wright and Creidhne the Metalworker, who forged magical weapons for the *Tuatha Dé* in their great battles against the *Fomhoire*. Driven out by the invading Celts, the *Tuatha Dé* established a realm beneath the earth, a mirror image, or Otherworld. From here they controlled the harvest and the flow of milk, so bargains had to be driven between the two worlds. At certain times of the year, princes, warriors and druids were permitted to visit the Otherworld, while gods and goddesses entered the human world in animal and spirit form, their ambiguity and shape-changing reflected constantly in Celtic art.

HERE WERE TWO FORMS OF EARLY GOLDWORK AMONGST THE insular Celts: in Britain, the goldwork of the Beaker and Food Vessel people, who arrived from Europe in 1,800 BC; and in Ireland the production of simple gold torques and neckrings from *c*. 1,400 BC. The Beaker people seem to have been a warrior aristocracy who established themselves on the existing people and were gradually absorbed. We know that they prized and loved gold. Gold basket-shaped earrings have been found at Radley in Oxfordshire and most striking of all is the fabulous Rillaton gold cup, found in a barrow in

Cornwall, which dates from 1,600 BC. Standing just 9cm high, with fluted and ribbed shape and riveted handle, it demonstrates the skill of these early metalworkers. It resembles Mycenean gold cups and trading links between Britain and the Mediterranean are not inconceivable. Chronologically parallel to the Beaker folk were the Food Vessel people of south and east Britain who produced simple gold torques and armlets of twisted gold – the best example being the Grunty Fen armlet torque, over 120cm of gold, twisted snake-like to run four times around the arm.

In Ireland, copper was used from 2,400 BC and was followed by bronze. Gold followed shortly afterwards – simple twisted neck torques of the Grunty Fen type, possibly dating from 2,000 BC, are not uncommon. The Irish developed their own skills, particularly in goldworking. The lunula is followed by more complex collars, the same moon-shape collar now featuring ribbed working and elegant terminals, which are decorated with sun circles and repoussé bosses.

Goibhniu, the Smith god, whose weapons always flew true and always killed on impact, one of a triad of craft gods, the others being Luchta the Wright and Creidhne the Metalworker, who were central to pagan Celtic society and culture. The figurine dates from the second century and shows how powerful the influence of Roman styles was in the north of England and near Hadrian's Wall.
MUSEUM OF ANTIQUITIES, NEWCASTLE UPON TYNE

Gold was not the only metal used. Bronze, a carefully calculated alloy of copper and tin, was worked from 1,700 BC. Tin was mined in south-west England, Cornwall, Wales, Scotland and Ireland and was of such value that it attracted traders from the Middle East and Greece. Amber, so revered and prized by the Celts through their pagan and Christian periods that it must have had particular symbolism, was imported from Europe.

Gold and bronze metalwork was being produced by the insular Celts from 1,600 BC, but it was the advent of the Iron Age, in the eighth century BC that marked the start of a period of rigorous expansion by the continental Celts and the two major artistic flowerings of Hallstatt in the sixth and La Tène in the fifth and fourth centuries BC. Iron, more plentiful and durable than bronze, and mined from shallow opencast sites, permitted a dramatic increase in weapon production.

Detail of the Ceremonial sceptre from the Sutton Hoo burial ship, early seventh century. The sceptre is the oldest surviving royal insignia ever to have been found in Britain. It is made of whetstone, the dense, heavy stone that was used to sharpen swords, and surmounted by a bronze stag which denotes its royal associations. Raedwald of East Anglia, who was buried in the Sutton Hoo ship, was probably a Saxon king but may have taken the sceptre as booty from a Celtic incumbent.
BRITISH MUSEUM

The earlier of the two European styles, Hallstatt, takes its name from an area of rock-salt deposits (from which salt could be extracted) high up in the Alps, in Upper Austria, some 305m above sea level. A large number of cremation graves indicate where the Celts established tribal colonies. The presence of a permanent settlement in one of the most inaccessible areas of the Alps show how important and valuable salt was, not only for taste but for preserving food. The site was abandoned in the fifth century, but many of the graves, including warrior and princely barrows, remained intact until they were excavated in the late nineteenth century. They revealed unexpected luxury and the prolific use of gold, bronze and precious stones.

The Hallstatt weaponry was decorated with a particular stylization of line, angular and geometric, sometimes in an inlay of Mediterranean coral, in chequerboard patterns. In its earliest form, decoration was quite functional involving simple cross-hatching, dots, compass arcs and triangles. To these rhythmic gyrations was added a repertoire of animal art: birds' heads, horses and wild dogs, distinctive swans and cygnets, crested waterbirds, cattle, stags and bulls. The gods had come to life on the weaponry, jewellery and figurines of the Celts.

ROSPEROUS AND BELLICOSE, THE CELTS PUSHED EAST AND SOUTH-EAST through Europe, marauding through the Balkans and settling new territories. They traded weapons and salt with the neighbouring Etruscans, hired themselves out as mercenaries to the northerly Greek states and set up commercial links as far afield as the Baltic to procure precious amber. By the fifth century BC a new style began to emerge around the area of the Middle Rhine. It has been called La Tène, from an area of a hundred or so rich barrow graves near Neuchâtel in Switzerland where it was first discovered. There is outstanding goldwork in the area of princely tombs, between the Rhine and the Meuse.

The La Tène style was complex and sophisticated, the work of skilled craftsmen working to the highest standards for princely and aristocratic patrons. Quite distinctive, its motifs, none the less, were borrowed and synthesized. From the Greeks came the combination of palmette and lotus buds, S-shaped lyres and the love of the arabesque or running line. From the Etruscans came a particular form of the human face: moustachioed, elongated and strong-browed, to which the Celts added their own variations – slit mouths and huge, voided eyes. Further afield, fantastic animals with lithe and sinuous bodies were imported from the folk art of the Steppe; the fondness for putting creatures in facing pairs came from the Persians; and from north Africa and India came the inspiration for exotic animals and foliage – tigers, lions, palm trees and lotuses.

A principal motif of La Tène is the wave tendril of Greek art, free-drawn triangles caught up in the running line of a wave which is just about to break. This was much admired by the Celts, appearing on brooches and sword scabbards throughout Celtic Europe. The wave tendrils of La Tène, combined with the simple foliage of the palmette, were initially used as a frieze, but were also ingeniously transmuted into an exquisite circular design. Later the La Tène style – often in relief work called repoussé – involved the use of snail-shell coils, dragon or griffin pairs, half-palmettes and 'trumpet' or 'comma' voids. Half-palmettes – tendrils crossing themselves in figures of eight – appear on the British Witham shield, made in the second century BC.

Compasses were used to create the most sensuous and fluent of La Tène work which was often so refined that many objects, such as horse trappings and gold open-work jewellery, appear as fretwork. Compass work also permitted the origination of the La Tène leaf motif, the so-called Waldesheim leaf, which was arranged in different combinations to create exquisite gold fretwork in which eyes, noses and moustaches magically appear and disappear. The gold bowl cover from Schwarzenbach in Saarland is a fine example.

Some of the most remarkable pieces that survive are a fusion of Hallstatt and La Tène styles, sword blades particularly showing a combination of animal Hallstatt and flowing La Tène. The pair of Basse Yutz flagons from the Moselle on the edge of the

Middle Rhine zone are a veritable directory of the respective design elements. From Hallstatt comes the coral chequer pattern underneath, and the plucky duck on top of the spout, while the four stylized lotus buds on the red enamel champlevé stopper are La Tène. La Tène, too, are the faces glimpsed two ways at the base of the handle and lcome datacompthe palmettes on the back of it. A Hallstatt dog or wolf arches over. The flagons were beaten out of a single sheet of bronze: the base was left open, and a collar of inlaid coral slipped over the bottom before a cast base was welded onto it. The spouts were then attached with rivets, and the lids, handles and rim animals added separately.

By the fourth century, at the height of the flowering of La Tène, the Celts dominated central Europe. In 397 BC they sacked Rome. In 358 BC they were in the Balkans, and a generation later Alexander the Great was forced to receive their envoys in the lower Danube. In the following century they overran Macedonia, plundered Apollo's temple at Delphi and by 270 BC had settled in large numbers on the Anatolian plateau near Ankara in Asia Minor, in the area called Galatae by the Romans. The Greeks finally vanquished them in 240 BC and at the Battle of Telamon in Italy in 225 BC it was the turn of the Romans. The following century the pressure of the Germanic and Teutonic people from the north, the Greeks from the east and the Romans from the south, who pressed into the Provence area of modern-day France, forced the Celts to consolidate their tribal areas. Scattered hillforts on the plains of Europe suited a people determined on expansion but, as their fortunes turned, they began to build large tribal settlements for the first time, which were called *oppida* by the Romans.

Gold openwork cover for a varnished bowl, from Schwazenbach, Saarland, fifth century BC, one of the treasures from a princely La Tène tomb. The basic motif is a leaf design, but arranged in such a way that eyes, noses and moustaches seem to appear from nowhere. Palmettes, the three-leafed designs like fleur-de-lys, are just visible towards the base of the bowls.
STAATLICHE MUSEEN ZU BERLIN

CELTIC BRITAIN

THE INSULAR CELTS OF ENGLAND, SCOTLAND AND WALES SHARED cultural and trading links with the continent throughout the Bronze and Iron Age periods and organized their society in more or less the same way. Britain has about 3,000 hillforts, many of which date from 1,300 BC and some, like Maiden Castle, show signs of habitation from 4,000 BC. Hillforts varied in size and purpose. Some were military and grain storage sites, occupied only in times of siege, the population otherwise living in small settlements in more accessible surroundings. Others, such as the magnificent Iron Age settlement at Stanwick in North Yorkshire, were virtually towns and built on a massive scale. Stanwick was a site of 850 acres encircled by 9.65 km of ramparts.

Bronze Battersea shield, dating from the first century BC, discovered in the river Thames half a mile or so upstream from present-day Westminster. Its great delicacy of design, which includes the inlay of red enamel, suggests it was a votive offering made to the river on the death of a king or warrior, or to ensure victory in battle.
BRITISH MUSEUM

While the basic style of art in Celtic Britain was La Tène in influence, it took on original styles and specializations in form depending upon the culture and traditions of each tribe. From the third century BC there was certainly a northern school of the Parisi and Brigantes tribes, an eastern school of the Iceni and a southern school of the fierce Belgae tribes, another branch of whom occupied the area across the Channel which is present-day Belgium and France. In Ireland, which the Romans never reached, the La Tène style had an unbroken development from the late Iron Age, its distinctive trumpets and spirals haunting the metalwork and manuscripts of the Christian period.

In Britain, red molten glass or champlevé enamel was often used as an ornament for jewellery, horse trappings, chariot mounts and arms, and it is found on both the Battersea and Witham shields. It is on account of the enamel that the earliest mention of the Celts of the British Isles is made, by the third-century BC chronicler, Philostratus: 'They say that the barbarians who live in the ocean pour colours on to heated bronze and that they adhere and grow hard as stone, keeping the designs that are made in them.' The insular Celts were also skilled weapon-smiths. Sheet bronze was made by casting an ingot and then beating it into a thin sheet, from which state it could be cut, moulded and decorated. Raised (repoussé) designs were made by hammering out shapes from behind, and were often used on shields. The advantage of the method was that the first piece could be used as a mould for a second sheet, hammered into it to create an identical design.

The insular metalworkers also practised a method of bronze casting called *cire-perdu*, or lost-wax casting, which was frequently used for casting solid torques or their heavy, decorated end terminals. The object was first modelled in wax and then encased in clay. The mould was heated to melt the wax, the clay was baked and then molten bronze, with a small amount of lead added to increase its pouring quality, was trickled in. After cooling, the clay mould was then broken to release the metalwork.

There were two kinds of society in first-century BC southern Britain, although both were agricultural. In the west and south-west, the Dumnonii tribe of Devon and Cornwall and the Dubunni of the Severn estuary functioned as merchant economies, wealth being gained by exchange rather than by military aggression. In the east and south-east, the Cantiaci of Kent, the Trinovantes of Essex and the Iceni of East Anglia were warlike, gaining wealth by plunder and conquest, slave trading and by hiring themselves out as mercenaries. In this period there were distinctions between western and eastern art, the metalworking skills of the eastern Celts being particularly assured and advanced both in ornate goldwork and weaponry.

Two shields and two shield bosses, all found in the east of the country, survive from the second and first centuries BC, a testament to the preoccupations of these fractious tribes. The so-called Battersea shield and the two Wandsworth shield bosses, found in the river Thames, probably belonged to the Cantiaci, the most culturally advanced of all Celtic tribes, who were settled in the London and Kent area. The Battersea Shield, dating from 75 BC and now housed in the British Museum, is made of bronze and indents gently into its middle, giving it a stunning 'waisted' symmetry. It features three roundels of high-relief beaten repoussé work, inlaid with red glass. Its great beauty and fragility would suggest that it was not used in battle, rather that it was a votive gift, deposited in water on the death of a warrior or as an offering to the gods. Of the two shields found in the Thames at Wandsworth, it is only the bosses, the central area of the shield that protected the handgrip, that survive. The first boss, circular and measuring 33 cm across, features two birds with curved beaks in flight, their wings and tail feathers brushing the circumference of the boss to form two halves of a circle. The second shield boss is oval, extending vertically to a man's head – a face elongated and stylized like a *Commedia dell'arte* mask – and has birds and rhythmic trumpet voids across three dimensions.

The Witham shield, found in the river Witham near Washington in Lincolnshire, belonged either to the Brigantes or Cirtani. It is earlier than the other three, probably dating from the second century BC, and is considered superior in technique to continental work of the same period. The outline of a wild boar can just be seen, its long limbs falling either side of a central coral-inlaid high-domed boss. This is entirely in keeping with descriptions of the time. Diodorus Siculus, writing between 60 and 30 BC

says: 'Their armour includes man-sized shields, decorated in individual fashion, some of these have projecting bronze animals of fine workmanship which serve for defence as well as decoration.' The shield seems to have passed through several generations or reincarnations – the boss has been riveted on and there is a range of motifs added at various times. The end circles are decorated with characteristic hair-spring spirals and split palmettes and at the centre of each is a flower motif, the whole supported by a horse's head within a lyre palmette, which is quite lovely.

Surprisingly, for the Iceni tribe of East Anglia were great warriors, it is not their military artefacts that have survived, but their treasure. From more or less the same period, *c.* 75 BC, comes the hoard of 183 gold, silver and bronze torques and bracelets from Snettisham in Norfolk, now thought to be the capital of the fierce Iceni prior to the Roman conquest. The site is at the northern end of the Icknield Way, near the Wash, and is guarded by four Iron Age fortresses.

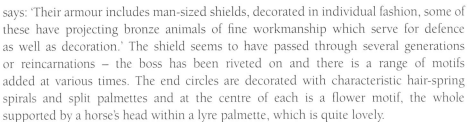

Bronze shield ornament from the river Witham in Lincolnshire, second century BC. The raised boss areas would have been beaten out from behind in the repoussé method. A central rosette is surrounded by simple chasing of S-shaped lyres with a half-palmette at either end. The horse's head below the roundel is typical of insular La Tène style.
BRITISH MUSEUM

To date, Snettisham has yielded the largest accumulation of precious metal from Iron Age Britain, and when it was discovered in 1991 it was the largest hoard of gold and silver treasure ever found, valued at £5–10 million. It was discovered in six pits hewn out of the rock, the huge quantities of accompanying precious metal scrap being buried in a copper cauldron which would have had symbolic and supernatural associations. It was a royal treasury and it reveals the great wealth of a ruling dynasty who, according to early accounts, took pride in wearing their gold into battle.

The same site produced one of the finest individual treasures of British Celtic history. The great ring-terminated Snettisham torque has been romantically associated with Boudica, Queen of the Iceni, who rose up in revolt and was defeated by the Romans in AD 60, although its style would suggest it was made a century before she lived. Dio Cassius, the Roman historian, nevertheless describes Boudica, 'huge of frame, terrifying of aspect, and with a harsh voice', with a great twisted golden necklace at her throat and we may assume that it was of a similar design. Weighing 1085 g, the Snettisham torque is a hoop of eight twisted strands, the ends terminating in two great ornate rings, decorated in the characteristic style of the Snettisham goldsmiths, with slender commas or trumpet coils and raised dots across three planes. It is one of a massive hoard of 61 torques, 2 bracelets and 158 gold coins found at the time: an extraordinary votive offering consigned to Mother Earth until such time as it might be needed.

A second hoard of torques was found at nearby Ipswich in the same tribal area. Although simpler in design – they are made from a long length of gold twisted and plaited back on itself – they are made from pure gold, and in the most meticulous way.

T IS NO WONDER THAT, SCENTING SUCH WEALTH, THE ROMANS EYED THE 'barbarians who lived in the ocean' and made plans for conquest.

In the course of a dogged eight-year campaign to subdue the Celts of Gaul, Caesar made two expeditions to Britain and received the nominal submission of southern leaders. Complete conquest, after the mammoth effort expended in the subjugation of Gaul, lay outside his grasp. However, he was impressed by the insular Celts and particularly struck by their method of careering into battle with chariots: 'First of all they drive in all directions and hurl missiles, and so by the mere terror that the teams inspire and by the noise of the wheels they generally throw ranks into confusion. When they have worked their way in between the troops of cavalry, they leap down from the chariots and fight on foot.' The Celts often fought naked, their bodies painted in woad, a strange blue dye.

By the early decades of the first century AD, the Catuvellauni and Trinovantes of the south-east were in regular contact with the Roman empire. Their king was the elderly Cunobelin, or Cymbeline (whose story Shakespeare was to tell nearly 1,500 years later), and he had two sons: Caratacos, fiercely anti- and Adminius slyly pro-Roman. Banished from the court at Colchester by his father, Adminius made for Rome, where he pledged allegiance to the emperor. It was just a matter of time before the invasion came. In AD 43 Emperor Claudius sent four legions, a force of 20,000 men, across Gaul to the neck of the Channel. They landed at Richborough, in the land of the Cantiaci, drove up across the river Medway in Kent and crossed the Thames to take the royal Trinovantes capital of Colchester. Caratacos fled to Wales. Adminius, by way of reward, was put on the Catuvellaunian throne, with its capital at St Albans.

From Colchester the Romans pushed out in three directions: north into the Fenland of the Iceni; due west toward the Severn estuary, the land of the Dubunni; and south west across southern Britain towards Devon and Cornwall into the land of the Dumnonii and Durotriques. Kingdoms fell at their feet: the proud Iceni in AD 47, the Atrebates of Dorset and Hampshire thirty years later. Just two rebellious queens stood in their way, Cartimandua of the Brigantes and Boudica of the Iceni. The former capitulated to Roman diplomacy, agreeing to settle with the emperor if she could reign in place of her husband at their capital at Stanwick in North Yorkshire. Boudica fought to her death in 60–61, reputedly taking poison rather than succumb to the Roman forces.

The Brigantes allowed Roman passage through their territory and it was from this base in AD 79 that general Agricola set out to conquer Scotland. He won a great victory against the Picts at Mons Graupius, just north of present-day Inverness, but it was insufficient to consolidate a Roman hold. They were never to conquer the whole of the British Isles, and by the end of the first century the frontier had pulled back to a line between the Solway Firth and the Tyne, later turned into a border by Hadrian's Wall.

It is only possible to imagine the meeting of the Celtic and Roman minds. Both cultures understood notions of honour, bravery and non-surrender; both cultures perceived the order of the world to be maintained by gods and goddesses; but while Celtic society was heroic, individualistic and even hedonistic, the Roman was highly structured, disciplined and organized, and nowhere was this more apparent than in their art. The fluidity, mysticality and ambiguity of image, which was the essence of Celtic art, was at odds with the rational, rather stolid, naturalistic Roman approach and initially it looked as if the Celtic might not survive.

From the outset the Romans were keen to distract Celtic metalworkers from the manufacture of tribal weaponry and chariots. In the south, Celtic art dutifully took on a more four-square appearance, straight lines, ordered friezes and regular die-stamping, replacing the distinctive one-off of the wax cast or repoussé work. In the west and south-west, which benefited by regular contact with Ireland – which the Romans did not reach – production in the old style was maintained. In the north, against all odds, Celtic art blossomed. The Brigantes began producing quantities of metalwork where there had been little, their numbers swelled by the smiths from the south who fled north. Four Celtic schools have been identified: one centred on the Iceni and Belgi in the south-east which was enthusiastic in its use of enamel; a big school in south Brigantia which was traditionally inclined but used new Roman techniques such as die-stamping; a lowland Scots school with some enamelling of lower quality and much raised boss work; and, north of the Clyde in the lands of the northern Picts, a school which specialized in massive armrings and horse-trappings.

Around Hadrian's Wall, completed in AD 123 and manned by garrisons of Roman infantrymen from all over the empire, something of a tourist art developed, since the Romans loved trinkets – brooches, boxes, rings, necklaces – and the Celts, with an eye to a market, easily adapted. Caskets, loved by the Romans, were unfamiliar to the Celts. None the less, a fine example of a casket mount found at Elmswell, Humberside, in the land of the Brigantes, dating from late in the first century AD combines lyre-palmette decoration with an (albeit stylized) Augustan vine pattern, and Roman berried rosettes. An abundance of these were produced around Hadrian's Wall. The Romans also introduced skillets, or little bowls with handles, which they called *paterae* and which soon received Celtic enamelled decoration. There was a particular style which grew up at Hadrian's Wall, sparkling with red, green and blue enamelling. Such articles were traded over the border to the north and seem to have become collectors' items in the south, examples being found as far afield as Amiens in the north of France.

Trinket art introduced new jewellery designs to the Celtic metalsmiths. Thistle brooches and S-shaped dragonesque shapes were copied from Roman models, but were decorated in a Celtic way, as if the metalsmith found the blank canvas irresistible. At Great Chesters on Hadrian's Wall, an Aesica brooch measuring some 10 cm was found dating from the second half of the first century, which resembles the Gallo-Roman thistle brooches of the Claudian period in shape but is pure Celtic in decoration – a flourish of lyre and tendrils in which the glimpsed heads of birds can be seen, and a face

at the bottom. The penannular or open-ringed brooch was also introduced by the Romans, from which descended the delicate and bejewelled brooches of the Irish school, of which the Tara brooch is one. The Romans brought new decorative effects as well. Filigree, the art of working fine wires of twisted gold and silver in curvilinear designs on to brooches, must have been learnt at this time and a technique called *millefiori*, which involved heating and twisting bundles of different-coloured glass rods, intrigued the Celts for the curvilinear designs that lay in the glass when it was sliced off.

Of great interest is the way the human face is portrayed under the Roman influence. The supernatural associations of the head for the Celts, their habit of taking severed heads into battle and the rather sinister sculptures which they produced offended the Romans. A bronze mask found at Cadbury Castle, one of the great Iron Age hillforts in the west of Britain, is an image of Medusa. Medusa was Greek in origin, not Celtic, but the cast would have been made by local metalworkers,

Tara brooch, mid-eighth century. An exquisite penannular of moulded bronze decorated with panels of interwoven filigree birds and beasts, tiny human heads and inlays of blue and red glass. It was a royal brooch and probably associated with the kings of Meath. Brooches replaced torques at the end of the Iron Age as the insignia of royalty.

TRINITY COLLEGE, DUBLIN

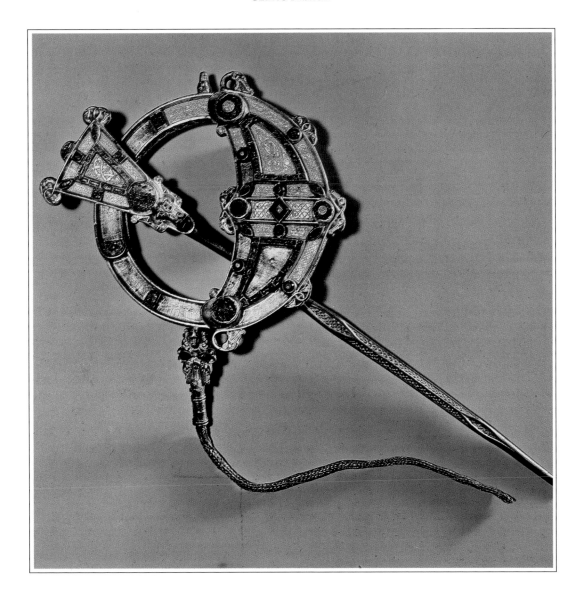

under duress, after the fort had been attacked in AD 73. Gone are the huge eyes, the long straight nose and elongated shape of Celtic features; the face instead is full-fleshed, squat-nosed, almond-eyed. Just a glimmer of the Celts remains in its slit mouth, a dour protest at the plumpness that surrounds it. A second-century statuette of Goibhniu the Celtic Smith god, found in the area of Hadrian's Wall, is almost without a trace of Celtic characteristics.

In the west the Celtic style won more frequently over the Roman. The great Celtic curative deity Sulis, whose hot springs at Bath gushed from the ground at a rate of a quarter of a million gallons a day, survived, her name kept intact into the Roman period. At Aquae Sulis, the water spewed through the open mouth of the stone-carved goddess, wild of hair and fierce of brow in the Celtic manner. A limestone sculpture of a male head, found in Gloucester, also survives from the first century and may have been intended as an honorific or funeral portrait of a Roman aristocrat. The Roman influence on it is clearly visible in the moulding of the head and the upward lift of the chin, but the features have been planed down to a superb Celtic mask, with bulbous eyes and long, thin nose.

ELTIC ARTISTRY, TENACIOUS TO THE LAST, DID SURVIVE. METALWORKERS bent themselves to Roman needs where necessary, but retained an identity which seems to have been tolerated, perhaps even admired by the Romans. On the whole the Roman influence was entirely beneficial. Roman glass, jewellery and pottery were more sophisticated and intricate than the Celtic and provided new models and insights into technique for the Celtic metalsmiths. When the Romans began to withdraw in the early fifth century, aspects of Roman technique and form that pleased the Celtic metalsmiths were retained while the use of mosaics and frescos, which were rather baffling to the Celts, were dropped. If there was damage done at all to Celtic artistry it was in the area of their weapon production.

Quelled by the Romans, constrained by the ban on the production of military artefacts, and softened by centuries of rule from the empire, the Celts had lost their belligerence and fighting spirit. This was to have dire consequences. The withdrawal of Roman troops from Britain in the early years of the fifth century left a vacuum and on the eastern coast Jute, Saxon and Angle warriors came in waves from the continent to wreak havoc on the hapless Celts.

The invasion ran the length of the eastern coastline and, unlike the Romans, who had wished only to impose order of Empire on the island beyond the sea and cull its wealth, the Anglo-Saxons came to settle on a permanent basis. The Celts, badly equipped and unused to fending for themselves, were displaced on a massive scale and driven west to Cornwall, Wales and into the west of Scotland. Here they were effectively trapped. Wales and Cornwall were subject to regular plunder by the Irish, increasingly practised raiders who came in search of slaves and booty. In despair some Celts in the sixth century, such as the monk Gildas, crossed the sea to Brittany, the only remaining refuge for them in Europe, rather than live with Saxon or Irish oppression.

HEN THE ROMANS DEPARTED, THEY TOOK WITH THEM THEIR scribes and chroniclers, and the Celts once again become the glimpsed people, appearing infrequently in written records until the eighth century. Despite the Roman withdrawal, on the west coast imported pottery shows that trading contacts established in the time of the Roman Empire remained intact. Tintagel Castle, the legendary birthplace of Arthur, sited on a rocky promontory on the northern coast of Cornwall was never conquered by the Romans, but seems to have enjoyed the benefits of proximity to the Roman trade routes. Excavations have produced quantities of late fifth-century (AD 480) pottery which shows that there were close links with the Mediterranean, and that Tintagel was a major British port of entry for goods and the main port of exit for Cornish tin, a commodity valued in the eastern Mediterranean. There are probably several thousand ceramic vessels in the castle including pots and bowls from Phocaea (western Turkey), tableware from Carthage (Tunisia), jars from Sardis (western Turkey), olive oil and wine amphorae from Cilicia (southern Turkey) and from the Peloponnese, all of which suggest a rather luxurious and sophisticated way of life for the inhabitants and not at all at odds with the picture of courtly life that appears in Arthurian legend.

There were five Celtic kingdoms in the Dark Ages: Gwynedd in north Wales, Powys which spread from mid-Wales into mid-England, Dumnonia in Devon and Cornwall, Gwent in south-east Wales and Dyfed in south-west Wales. It has been suggested that a great warrior called Owain Ddantgwyn may have ruled Powys in the latter part of the fifth century and was known honorifically in battle as *arth* or Bear. No direct references to Arthur, king of the Britons, survive and those that do are elliptical. Mons Badonicus or the Battle of Badon, which halted the Saxons in their tracks, took place for sure in the late fifth or early sixth century but it is not known where. Bede records the date as 493 and mentions it as a crushing defeat for the Saxons. The Celtic monk Gildas writing in Wales in 545 describes it, with great passion, as 'almost the last slaughter wrought by us on that scum of the earth' (he meant the Saxons), adding that now the Saxon blaze had spread 'until it licked the western ocean with its fierce red tongue'.

The significance of the stories of Arthurian legend is that, despite being laundered into a more Christian shape, they do, in elements, reflect Celtic life in late Iron Age society. The magical properties of Arthur's sword Excalibur are in accord with Celtic belief: as a boy Arthur draws it from the stone in which it is embedded, proof of his legitimate kingship; as a young man he retrieves it from the middle of a lake; on his death, it is thrown back into the lake as a votive offering. The detail of the Round Table, with one seat left vacant, reserved for the knight who would complete the quest for the Holy Grail, was added by Wace, a Norman cleric in the thirteenth century. But the practice of sitting in a circle was recorded by the early Roman chroniclers and seems to have been a feature of early Celtic society: 'When a large number dine together,

they sit around in a circle with the most influential man in the centre . . . whether he surpass the others in warlike skill or nobility of family or wealth. Beside him sits the host and next to either side the others in order of distinction.'

The Arthurian legends are the most modern of a body of Welsh tales, written down from the tenth century, known now as the *Mabinogi*. All tell of heroic supernatural beings, the equivalent of the *Tuatha Dé* whose divinity is not immediately apparent. There are enchanted animals, heads that speak even when separated from the body, the metamorphosis from animal to human form and back again, and cauldrons capable of resurrecting the dead. The Underworld is called Annwn, presided over by Arawn and his dazzling white hounds (white always signifying the supernatural in Celtic tales).

Irish myths have the advantage of being written down from the sixth century and have been shown by archeology to be reliable guides to Celtic society, culture and belief in the Iron and Dark Ages. The themes are similar to the Welsh: the sanctity of water, magic cauldrons of plenty, the significance of three, magic birds, possession of wealth and status symbols, but they have a more powerful fertility element.

Half of the Old Irish tales came from Ulster, which seems to have had a population, perhaps of the same origin as the Picts, which was pre-Celtic. One of the ancient kingdoms of Ireland, it formed, with Connaught in the west, Munster in the south, Leinster in the east, and Meath in the east midlands, one of the 'fifths' of Ireland. The royal capital was the Emain Macha, a hillfort, still visible, a few miles from the ecclesiastical capital of Armagh.

The Ulster Cycle, which includes *Táin Bó Cuailngne*, or the Cattle Raid of Cooley, has elements which are very old. All the characters who pass through the stories have supernatural elements. The brazen Medhbh, queen of Connaught, who cuckolds her husband with the Ulster Hero Ferghus mac Roich, is in fact a goddess of the land and its sovereignty, and her function is to mate with those who deserve kingship and to cast aside those who do not. The young Ulster warrior Cú Chulainn singlehandedly defends Ulster against the Connaught men. And the great brown bull of Cooley represents power and fertility, the quest for which is at the centre of *Táin Bó Cuailngne*.

Mingled into these tales are the essential ingredients of heroism, love, and risk, but at their root they concern sovereignty and rightful kingship. Ireland's 'fifths' were always at each other's throats, and each took ascendancy at some point during the Iron Age. By the end of the second century AD, a king called Conn Ced-Cathach, or Conn of the Hundred Battles, founded a dynasty which combined Meath and Connaught. His successors claimed a mythical overlordship of Ireland for the next thousand years, called themselves *Ard Ri*, or the High Kings of Ireland, and used as their royal seat Tara, a bleak hill some twenty miles north of present-day Dublin. By the third century Conn's grandson Cormac Mac Airt had imposed rule over a third of Ireland. In the fourth century the kingdoms of Ireland were upset, once again, by the dominance of one particular dynasty. The Ui Néill family were originally part of Connaught's ruling families, the descendants of Conn of the Hundred Battles, and they began a period of

Fuller Fibula, sixth or seventh century. Saxon brooches, unlike the delicate penannulars of the Celts, were solid circular affairs decorated in a rhythmic and symmetrical manner. Here a whimsical Celtic influence is shown in the expressions on the faces, while Roman dress and mannerisms are evident in the figures.
BRITISH MUSEUM

rapid expansion. Niall of the Nine Hostages, Lord of the Ui Néill, set his sights on Ulster and within a generation had all but gobbled it up. Further afield he raided Wales and the west coast of Scotland. It was his successors who finally created an Irish kingdom across the sea. They called it East Gael, or Argyll.

A ninth-century collection of aphorisms called *The Wisdom of Cormac the Wise*, surely overlaid with Christianity, provides an insight into royal interests in this period. 'Among the best things for a king', Cormac announces, 'are firmness without anger, keeping hostages in fetters, honouring poets, importing treasure from over the sea, and an abundance of wine and mead.' It is not difficult to picture the way of life during the Dark Ages. Trade with the continent brought in goods of some luxury, particularly Cormac's abundance of wine, for which the Celts had gained a taste under the Romans. Cattle-rustling, hunting, feasting, the telling of epic tales, the arrangement of dynastic marriages, must all have occupied a great deal of time. The importing of treasure from over the sea is a curious allusion, but may have referred to the detailed and fine metalwork being produced under Roman influence in the north of England, which the Irish undoubtedly coveted.

Brooches, part of the Celtic repertoire from the Iron Age, were produced in Ireland in some intricacy in the seventh, eighth and ninth centuries. They were associated with kingship and warrior status, the most ornate were effectively a form of crown jewels, and in this respect successors to the Iron Age torques. They were worn differently by men and women, a distinction which is referred to in an Irish law tract relating to accidental injury from projecting pins, which makes reference to the fact that men wore brooches on their shoulders, women on their breast.

The penannular shape was adopted from the Roman model and adapted and refined by Irish metalsmiths to include a great deal of enamelwork and adroit handling of semi-precious stones, millefiori and filigree. During the seventh century the techniques of metalwork were dramatically enhanced. Casting achieved a remarkable fineness; inlays of enamel and millefiori glass became more complex; gilding was used extensively on silver and bronze; and filigreework grew more assured and versatile. Inlays of niello

and amber extended the decorative range of the craftsmen. There were specialized crucibles for smelting gold and silver, techniques to create gold and silver mesh wire, and with the techniques came the potential for new designs. Roman withdrawl from the north of England and the expansion of the Irish Ui Néill dynasty into Argyll on the west coast of Scotland, brought an artistic and cultural union to the area. Many brooch moulds have been found at Dunadd, the seat of the kings of the Scottish Dal Riada, or Argyll, and finds of Pictish treasure, such as that of St Ninian's Isle, feature silver pinless brooches of great style.

The two great brooches of the later period, the Hunterston and the Tara, represent the height of the metalworker's art and the two main centres of production. Both were substantial in size. The Hunterston measures 11.1 cm × 11.8 cm in diameter, a flattened closed ring of a favourite Pictish medium, silver, with part of its pin missing. It is divided by ridges into panels, filled with animal interlace, spirals and trumpets, all described and emboldened in filigree. Smaller panels are set with amber studs. It is an unusually composed work, no space is overworked, no detail ill-conceived, and its splendour would suggest a royal or noble patron. That it did not stay within the family for which it was intended can be understood clearly from the back, where two claims of ownership are written in runic Scandinavian letters: 'Olfriti owns this brooch' is one, 'Maelbritha owns this brooch' the other. They were added in the tenth century when the brooch had fallen into Norse hands.

The Tara brooch, smaller than the Hunterston, at 8.7 cm in diameter, follows the same basic design, but miraculously the pin is intact. An exquisite penannular, it possibly formed one of a pair designed to be worn on the shoulder as the fastener for a cloak, but more likely it was a status symbol, to be seen rather than worn. The ring is of moulded bronze and, unlike the Hunterston, is decorated front and back. On both sides the surface is decorated with panels, large and small, in which interwoven filigree birds and beasts, tiny human heads carved in amethyst, and inlays of blue and red glass are worked with extraordinary skill. It dates from the mid-eighth century and was found not at Tara, but in a wooden box on a beach in County Meath. It is not known to whom it belonged, but the assumption has been that because of the quality of the work it must be a royal brooch.

Although these two brooches express the height of technical and artistic achievement in this period, they are far from being the only examples. Annular brooches continued to be produced in Ireland until the ninth century, with a much greater use of Germanic

Hinged gold shoulder clasps from the Sutton Hoo burial ship, early seventh century. Germanic cloisonné work, of which the jewelled and enamelled interior is an example, was practised with a high degree of skill in East Anglia. The influence of the design of the clasps has been noted on the carpet pages of the Book of Durrow.
BRITISH MUSEUM

animal interlace along the margins of the rings. In Scotland the brooches never went out of fashion. Often of plain silver, and now decorated in the Anglo-Saxon and Viking way with single animals, their association with kingly status survived well into the medieval period.

BACK IN SOUTHERN BRITAIN, CONDITIONS IN THE FORMER CELTIC homelands after the Saxon invasions seem not to have hampered the metalsmith. There was a modest renaissance of production, of which one of the main features was the manufacture of hanging bowls in the sixth and seventh centuries. There has been much argument about their origins and purpose, but these simple bowls made of beaten or spun bronze with their vividly enamelled escutcheons (the circular plaques which held the rings by which the bowls were hung) seem somehow central to the survival of Celtic art in the Dark Ages. They were made particularly in Northumbria, Scotland and west England and Ireland and are found in both Celtic and Saxon graves. By the seventh century a great deal of work went into the escutcheons: the use of two colours without a division of metal, and sophisticated use of triskeles, trumpet shapes, palmettes, coils, commas and leaf motifs. It is as if they were the preparation and training for the great effort of Christian art which was now imminent and it is possible that their earliest models were Byzantine chalices or lamps which had religious functions.

By all accounts the hanging bowls were traded with the Saxons and Celtic metal-smiths may even have returned to the east of the country. Celtic art with its curvilinear patterns, enamel and millefiori inlays was in direct contrast to the rigid animal style of the Anglo-Saxons, but a gradual meshing of the two styles began to take place. Its first and most interesting expression is found in the burial ship of Sutton Hoo, the remark-able and strange tomb of the East Anglian king Raedwald, who died in 624. Raedwald was probably a Saxon king, but amongst the treasures buried with him are three Celtic hanging bowls, thought to be old when placed there as they had been repaired by Saxon metalsmiths, and a massive Celtic cauldron, symbol of resurrection and rebirth, with an astonishing ironwork chain. Here, too, is Raedwald's sceptre, the oldest insignia of royalty ever found in Britain. It is made of whetstone, which is redolent of Celtic design and execution, and may have been snatched as booty two centuries earlier by the invading Anglians.

The jewellery buried at Sutton Hoo is of some interest too. A pair of hinged shoulder clasps, made of gold and decorated with garnets, mosaic glass and filigree, bespeak Celtic influence. The knotwork interlace on the gold belt buckle appears again, later in the century, on the carpet pages of the Book of Durrow, and the animal interlace, which appears on a purse top, was also destined to appear in Celtic religious art. Significantly, the ship contains artefacts of both Christian and pagan burial, and two altars were found side by side within it. A great Byzantine silver dish nods in the direction of Christianity. Delightfully, forty gold coins, forged in Merovingian Gaul, acknowledge the pagan need, as in Greek mythology, to pay the ferryman.

CHRISTIAN GOLD

AT THE HEIGHT OF ITS INFLUENCE, AND UNDER MEN SUCH AS PATRICK, Columba of Iona, David of Wales, Aidan of Lindisfarne and Columbanus of Luxeuil and Bobbio, the Celtic or Irish Church dominated western Europe and guarded its Christian tradition for the centuries between the decline of the Roman Empire and the revival of the Roman Church in the seventh century. Its territories extended from Ireland in the far west, through the north of Scotland to the Northumbrian monastic settlements at Lindisfarne, Melrose, Jarrow, Whitby and Durham, south to Kent, across the Channel to the lands of the Merovingian Franks, east into the Germanic lands and even further beyond; there was a Celtic

'Carpet' Page, folio 94, Lindisfarne Gospels, c. 698. The perfect symmetry of the page could not have been achieved without meticulous planning and superb compass work, both of which were a feature of the Lindisfarne scriptorium. The circular cross at the centre of the page became a model for stone crosses in Northumberland, Scotland and Ireland.
BRITISH LIBRARY

monastic settlement at Kiev until the twelfth century when it was destroyed by the Mongol advance from the East.

The energy and commitment of the men of the Celtic Church directed the production, to the glory of God, of some of the great artworks of the early Western Church. To them are due the brilliant manuscript folios of Durrow, Lindisfarne and Kells, the sophisticated church metalwork of Ardagh and Darrynaflan, and the creation of a composite school of artistic expression which marked the transition of Celtic art from the Dark Ages into a fully fledged, early European medieval style.

If the impetus behind this Celtic renaissance was the coming of Christianity to the insular regions of Ireland and Britain, what could not have been predicted was the artistic and intellectual response of the Celts to the new religion which was prodigious and effervescent. Their ability to absorb style and substance from other art forms – in the Bronze Age from classical Greece and Persia, later from the Romans and Etruscans – and make it their own, was proven again in the Christian period. They studied, assimilated and synthesized the Coptic religious art of the Middle East, the complex interwoven animal art of the Saxons, and the naturalistic style of the Picts to produce an artistic fusion, recognizably Celtic, and bursting with colour and life.

Their technical achievements, too, were manifold. They learnt, for the first time in their artistic culture, to draw and paint. They created an elegant and simple written hand, the Celtic uncial and half-uncial. They developed and perfected the art of the elongated and majesterial initial capital letter which swayed and danced on the page; and they produced mathematically exact designs of pure decoration in their sacred texts, the so-called cross carpet pages.

At the great Irish monasteries – Bangor, Clonmacnois, Clonfert, Moville, Clonard, Kildare, Glendalough – and at Iona and Lindisfarne, and their daughter foundations at Melrose, Jarrow, Durham and Whitby, there was a passion for learning which was equalled only by the Greeks and Romans. Men such as Columba were early renaissance men, versed in the classics, but also knowledgeable about poetry, history and literature. At Lindisfarne mathematics, grammar and physics were taught. In Ireland the ancient tales of the Celts were written down for the first time. The Celtic Church drew no lines between the gospel texts, classical literature and their own oral tradition. The monasteries became early universities, with Christ, as one historian has aptly described it, 'as a sort of liberal chancellor', who allowed the study of the non-religious.

HRISTIANITY WAS FIRST INTRODUCED TO BRITAIN (ALTHOUGH NOT TO Ireland) by the Romans in the second and third centuries. It must have spread rapidly and with gusto since a reference is made from North Africa, by a Roman scribe, Tertullian, writing around AD 200, that the word of Christ had reached parts of Britain beyond Romanized areas (*Britannorum inaccessa Romanis loca Christo vero subdita*). By 240 another chronicler, Origen, observed that it was a force which was unifying the Britons. Apart from the urban centre there were pockets of Christianity in Galloway, Wales, Cornwall, north-east Britain and even Ireland.

The world of the pagan Celts meshed well with the new religion. Monasteries unashamedly flourished on old Celtic religious sites. Bede describes Durrow as 'a noble monastery in Ireland known in the Scots (Irish) language as Dearmach, the Field of Oaks, because of the oak forest in which it stands'. Oaks, of course, were the sacred trees of the druids. Columba chose Kells, which had been a prehistoric burial site and a hillfort associated with the southern Uí Néill, as his second monastic foundation in Ireland. Often, when there were no ancient sites to be had, the new monasteries were planned just like Iron Age hillforts anyway with the addition of a church of stone or wood. Monasticism itself, at the heart of the Celtic Church, with its concerns of community and kinship, fitted seamlessly into the powerful territorial and familial society of the Celts. Even the Celtic tonsure, shaved from ear to ear over the top of the head and growing long at the back, was more druidical than Christian in appearance.

For all this the sincerity – and austerity – of monastic life was without doubt. Both Iona and Lindisfarne (the first monastic site on mainland Britain) were built upon exposed islands. Lindisfarne was prey to the icy east winds that swept in from the Baltic, Iona to the turbulent and unpredictable tides of the Irish sea. When Columba and his twelve followers landed on Iona in 563 they built simple wattle monastic cells, a barn, farm buildings, kiln and mill, traces of which remain, but which must have been scant comfort in the long winters. Columba, like his fellow monks, slept on a rock for his bed. The pattern was repeated at Lindisfarne, first by Aidan, who founded it in 635, and subsequently by Cuthbert, who retreated as a hermit to the island of Inner Farne.

HE CELTS, ALWAYS GREAT AND EXPANSIVE STORYTELLERS, SPUN the bare facts about their early religious fathers into their myth and legend and, in so doing, enhanced the mystique of the church. The early saints were endowed with supernatural powers familiar to the Celts: miraculous births, living to advanced ages, magical journeys and powerful voices. There was Brendan, the sailor saint and founder of the great monastery of Clonfert, who set sail for seven years with thirty monks on a sort of Homeric odyssey, to find spiritual enlightenment, and whose mythical island, St Brendan's Isle, the Land of

The Calf, symbol of St Luke, folio 124, Book of Durrow, 650–675. The image owes much to Pictish art, which was more naturalistic than the Celtic. The fore and hindleg joints are picked out with great care and closely resemble those of the dog whose arching body forms the handle of the Basse-Yutz flagons made some thousand years previously.
TRINITY COLLEGE, DUBLIN

Promise, became the Gaelic Atlantis, a lost world somewhere in the Atlantic mists. There was, too, Finnian of Clonard, Brendan's monastic settlement in Leinster, revered for his learning and known as 'tutor of saints of Ireland', whose youth had been spent at St David's foundation in Pembrokeshire in Wales.

Bestriding them both was Columba, father of the Irish Church in Scotland, founder of the great monasteries at Iona, Durrow and Kells, and Prince of the Uí Néill, whose singing voice was 'melodious and extraordinarily powerful' and could, apparently, be heard at a distance of four, sometimes eight furlongs. Given the name Colum at birth, he became *Colum Cille*, Colum of the Church, and Columba or 'dove' in Latin. Although the establishment of Iona under royal protection and prerogative clothed a political as well as a religious mission to convert the Northern Picts, he was a devout and humble man. He died at the altar of his church, in 597 aged seventy-six, the year that Augustine landed at Canterbury bringing a revival of the Roman Church.

Finally, there was Columbanus, 'perhaps the most dynamic personality the Celtic church has produced', who pushed the influence of Irish Christianity deep into the lands of the Merovingian Franks and the Lombards and sowed the seeds for the foundation of ninety-four continental monasteries in France, Germany and Flanders, many of which, although under Benedictine rule, remained thriving communities throughout the Middle Ages. He had been educated in Bangor, but left with twelve companions for France, founding a monastery first in the rocky wilderness of Luxeuil in the Vosges mountains and then at Bobbio in Italy in 612. Although his monasteries became cosmopolitan, Columbanus's first love was solitude and quiet communion with nature. He talked, so the legend went, with birds and beasts on equal terms, an early St Francis of Assisi in the Celtic mould.

T HE NEED TO POSSESS WEALTH, A DRIVING FORCE FOR THE pre-Christian Celts as a sign of kingship and status, was just as important in the Christian era and the paraphernalia and accoutrements of Christianity were taken very seriously. The new churches required sacred vessels for the Eucharist, chalices for wine, plates for communion bread, books, wine strainers, lamps, bells, bookcovers, bindings, vestments, altar cloths, coffins and later stone crosses for burial. Early missionaries could not have carried a great deal, but Patrick's seventh-century biographer Tírechán is adamant that he brought with him across the river Shannon: 'fifty bells, fifty patens, fifty chalices, altar stones, books of law, and books of gospels' and left them in 'new places'. 'For the church which has not its proper equipment is not entitled to the dues of God's Church, and is not a church but its name according to Christ is a den of thieves,' states an eighth-century text entitled *The Rule of Patrick*.

While the production of metalwork had a secular basis, the illumination of manuscripts was sacred work, produced by scriptoria, or groups of skilled monks, within the monasteries. *De Abbatibus* tells also of an Irish scribe called Ultán, the bones of whose hands were revered as sacred relics because he had inscribed the words of God.

In the mythology of the early Church, the earliest of the Irish manuscripts, the Cathach or Psalter of Columba, was transcribed by the hand of Columba himself and was of such sanctity that it was carried into battle at the head of the army of O'Donnell in 1497. Columba died in 597 and while it is possible that he had access

to a manuscript of psalms to copy, a later date for the transcription is more probable, when the trickle of manuscripts from the East found their way into the continental monasteries of the Irish Church and then back to the Irish foundations. Although the Cathach is undecorated, it has two features of the later gospel books: the first hint of decorated initial letters, along the Coptic model, and the use of red dots to highlight these letters, which gives them a three-dimensional appearance.

The Church's missionaries, whether Celtic or Roman, had understood from the beginning the importance of decoration. Pope Gregory the Great in the sixth century explained that the images provided 'a living reading of the Lord's story for those who cannot read'; while, according to Bede, the first thing that St Augustine brought to England in 597 was a silver cross and an 'image of our Lord and Saviour painted on a panel'. The need to impress the unconverted was just as powerful in the eighth century, when St Boniface, a British missionary to the Germans, commissioned from the Abbess of Minster in Thanet the Epistles of St Peter to be written out in gold (he would supply the gold), that he might 'impress honour and reverence for holy scripture before the eyes of the carnal in his preaching'. For the Celts, the power of the new religion, which came with books and bells mysteriously inscribed with symbols, must have been quite overwhelming.

The skills needed to produce manuscripts were new to the Celts: the transformation of cattle and sheep skins into quality vellum, the handling of quill and brush, the forming of written letters. Much must have been absorbed simply by examining Eastern manuscripts with their simple palette of colours, the use of the proud initial letter and the careful blend of knotwork and interweave on the carpet pages which preceded the beginning of each gospel.

The Lion, symbol of St Mark, folio 19, Book of Durrow, 650–675. The Celtic artist painted the lion on a plain white background using great restraint. The head of the lion is Germanic, his torso belongs to Pictish art.
TRINITY COLLEGE, DUBLIN

There were two sorts of gospel books: the highly decorated books of Lindisfarne, Kells and Durrow which were intended for the altars of the largest monasteries, and simple pocket books in a cursive or informal hand for the smaller communities and private devotion. Since every monastic community must have had one or more of the pocket books, the scriptoria must have been constantly busy. The pocket books have long since perished, but many of the illuminated manuscripts have survived more or less intact.

Although they vary in style and artistic influence, there are similarities between them. They all used as their model the gospel text based on the Vulgate translation of the Bible by St Jerome in 384, examples of which would have circulated in the continental Celtic monasteries from the end of the sixth century and eventually found their way to the main monasteries in Ireland. What distinguishes the St Jerome Vulgate version is the order of the evangelists: Matthew, Mark, Luke and John, not, as in earlier gospels, the old order of Matthew, John, Luke and Mark.

With the exception of the Book of Kells, where decoration spills giddily from page to page, the gospel manuscripts stick to a fairly rigid form. Each gospel is announced by a symbol of the evangelist; a highly decorated 'carpet' page or 'cross carpet' page, so called because the pages, constructed with great mathematical care, resemble the carpet designs of the East but bear the Christian cross; and a highly decorated initial letter. All make much of the symbols of the apostles and the start of each gospel proudly displays their images: a man (Matthew), a lion (Mark), a calf or ox (Luke) and an eagle (John). St Gregory in his homilies explains the symbols as stages in Christ's life – he was born a man, was a calf in his death, a lion in his resurrection and an eagle when he ascended to Heaven, which – with all its shape-shifting – must have had a delightful resonance with the Celts.

The manuscripts are written on quality vellum and in the insular half-uncial, or half-inch script, which developed in Britain and Ireland under the influence of Christian missionaries from Rome. The vellum would have been taken from royal and monastic herds. The Lindisfarne Gospels, written on 130 sheets, 50 cm wide, folded

into 259 leaves, would have needed several herds. The Book of Kells, with its 185 sheets, used even more. Probably the production of a major book would have been well planned, and word sent out to affiliated monasteries, princes and kings for contributions. The skins were prepared by soaking in lime to dissolve their hair, then stretched, scraped clean and allowed to dry before being trimmed and bound together as pages. Celtic scribes used the suede side of the vellum (the opposite side to the continent) which was receptive to colour and ink.

The earliest examples of insular half-uncial are the Springmount Bog Tablets, now in the National Museum of Ireland, which date from 580. The Celtic half-uncial was a large rounded hand in which the words ran on, without punctuation or spaces between them. It became particularly refined at Lindisfarne at the time of transcribing the gospels. Insular script was voluptuously rounded – the e was enclosed instead of a greek e, the g had a curly tail, the x extended its tails curvaceously. Letters were topped with flying pennants. The script was employed subsequently by masons on memorial stones and crosses. Pens were cut from swan or goose quills or from reeds, and black carbon ink was made from soot dissolved in water. Kells, however, mainly used a brownish ink made from crushed oak apples and sulphate of iron in a medium of gum and water.

There is little or no decoration in the earliest manuscripts and what there is is limited to the decoration of their capital letters in red and yellow, colours which were also favoured in champlevé enamel. Reflected in the manuscripts were the colours of the

natural world that surrounded the monks: brown, green, red and a yellow the colour of gorse appeared autumnally on Durrow's pages. The blue and mauve of the hills of Mull and Scotland influenced the Iona scriptorium. Although some colours could be extracted from natural vegetation, many of them had to be imported, presumably at great expense. Blues were derived from woad or the oriental plant indigo; organic mauves, maroons and purples probably came from the Mediterranean plant *Crozophora tinctoria*; yellow came from orpiment or yellow arsenic sulphide; red and white were obtained from lead and vermilion from the pregnant body of an insect native to the Mediterranean called *kermoccocus vermilio*; green came from copper; and, most expensive and difficult to obtain of all, a deep blue was made from lapis lazuli, only available from a mine in north-east Afghanistan. All were mixed with egg white and applied with brushes made from the fine animal hair of rodents.

In all the gospel texts there are elliptical allusions to pagan Celtic imagery which would have been well understood by both the converted and the unconverted. The spirals and commas of La Tène appear with new vigour in the decoration of capital letters and there is consistent use of bird imagery. The Celts loved all birds, which they regarded as sacred messengers of the Otherworld, but particularly crested waterbirds – cranes, cormorants and herons – because they belonged to all the elements: air, water and land. Birds are woven together in the carpet pages of the Lindisfarne and Lichfield books on an invisible grid of pagan Ss. The wrought-iron suspension chain of the great

Sutton Hoo cauldron is evoked in the striking drop capital I of the *In Principio* (In the beginning) of the Durrow and Lindisfarne manuscripts; and the hounds or dogs interwoven in the books of Kells and Lindisfarne are old pagan motifs of the Dalriada tribe of ancient Ulster to which Columba belonged.

Familiar, too, would have been the doodles and asides on the manuscripts. On the initial page of Luke in the Lindisfarne Gospels, a cat forms a border around the page, with eight rather surprised birds inside it, and it has such a fixed and determined expression on its face that it must be sizing up a ninth on the opposite carpet page. The Celtic love of nature was everywhere. 'Wondrous is the robin there singing to us, and our cat has escaped,' a monk has written in a margin. In the Book of Kells cats chase mice; mice fight over communion wafers; lizards bask in the sun. The Celtic feel for animals and the natural world was unique.

The complexity of the work on the illuminated pages has created much debate about the amount of time they must have taken to produce. Seventy-eight birds are woven into the carpet page of John in the Lindisfarne Gospels, each mathematically and artistically perfect. The 10,600 dots of red lead on the Luke initial of the Lindisfarne Gospels must have taken days to put in, and for some of the illuminated initial and carpet pages in the Book of Kells one can only imagine weeks, perhaps months of labour.

While the origins of the insular manuscript tradition were Irish, many other influences were brought to bear and the synthesizing of art from other cultures is one of the predominant features. Apart from indigenous Celtic roundels and swirls, many of which are similar to the hanging bowl escutcheons of the post-Roman period, Germanic, Coptic, Persian, Greek and Pictish motifs are much in evidence. In the canon tables, chains of birds walk up and down the arch and columns, copied directly from manuscripts such as the Syrian Rabbula Gospels, of which they were a great feature, and from the bird processions of Syrian and Persian textiles. Motifs of dots and ribbon interlace were of Coptic origin. Peacocks and fish derive from the great tradition of Byzantine art, while wolves and eagles were absorbed from the naturalistic art of the Picts.

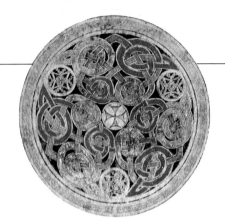

THE HOLY BOOKS OF GOLD

FOR SHEER VISUAL BEAUTY AND HARMONY, THE EARLIEST OF THE COMPLETE gospel manuscripts, the Book of Durrow, is without match. It is a poised, elegant work, modest in its proportions – measuring just 24 cm × 16 cm – aglow with the simple autumn colours which must have befitted its foundation, Columba's 'fields of oak', but with a reserve and sense of space which are harder to find in later manuscripts. The Celts, like nature, abhorred a vacuum, but imitation of the Syrian and Coptic manuscripts helped to restrain them in this instance, and the images that were produced, on the carpet pages and the pages of evangelist symbols, have a wonderful stillness on their plain white backgrounds.

'Carpet' Page, folio 192, Book of Durrow, 650–675. 'Carpet' pages, with a cross at the centre, were a feature of the Celtic insular manuscripts. This one, aglow with the simple autumn colours which were a feature of the Durrow manuscript, shows Germanic influences in its animal interlace. The central roundel is Celtic and resembles the escutcheons of contemporary hanging bowls.
TRINITY COLLEGE, DUBLIN

Durrow had been founded in 585 when the Abbot of Iona temporarily broke off from his evangelization of the Picts and sailed to Ireland to establish a daughter foundation. Despite its name, it is not known if the manuscript was compiled at Durrow or in the scriptorium at Iona. The book was made between 650 and 675, before the emergence of the powerful Northumbrian scriptoria, but after the foundation of the monasteries at Jarrow, Melrose, Whitby, Ripon and Lindisfarne.

Whoever worked on it and wherever it was produced, it is a work of considerable charm and reflects perfectly the 'new style' of Celtic artistry in its combination of Coptic, Germanic, Pictish and indigenous Celtic designs. Two of these give the Durrow book its particular feel: the Coptic, in the carpet pages and knotwork, and the Pictish in the evangelist symbols of St Luke and St Mark. The calf or ox of St Luke is tenderly portrayed, its thigh and shoulder joints meticulously picked out, so that they look rather like prize rosettes. Imitation of the Coptic produced the first semi-figurative portrait in Celtic art, that of Matthew in his bell-shaped gown, two feet sticking out of the bottom, looking as if he rightly belonged in a later Persian miniature. His robe of broad geometrical design is reminiscent of the chequerboard coral inlay of the Hallstatt wine flagons. His mouth is a characteristically Celtic slit; his hair seems almost beyond explanation, its tonsure being neither Celtic nor Roman.

The Durrow manuscript has intrigued scholars because of its parallels with the Sutton Hoo treasure. The carpet pages, rich with knotwork, closely resemble the ornate gold belt plate, while the animal interlace of the carpet page has a strong Germanic

The earliest portrait of a man ever made in Celtic art: the symbol of St Matthew, folio 21, Book of Durrow, 650–675. He wears a bell-shaped chequered gown whose design has something in common with the shoulder clasps of Sutton Hoo. The feet show Eastern influences and the image would probably have been copied from a Coptic or Syrian manuscript. The slit mouth is distinctively Celtic.
TRINITY COLLEGE, DUBLIN

flavour and elements of it could be taken from Sutton Hoo jewellery. In its groupings of three roundels of the same colours the central knot echoes the Celtic hanging bowl escutcheons found within the burial ship, and particularly striking is another hanging bowl analogy: the *In Principio* at the beginning of St John's gospel features a wonderful drop capital I for which parallels have been drawn with the wrought-iron suspension chain of the great Sutton Hoo cauldron. The chequerboard millefiori of the evangelist Matthew harks back to the work on the Sutton Hoo shoulder clasps, and the animal interlace of the Durrow carpet page has strong links with the decorative jewellery beasts. And yet thirty-five to fifty years, and hundreds of miles, separate the two. How was it possible? Similar artwork would have been produced in the eastern provinces of Britain on a continuous basis and we know that the Irish were visitors to the Anglian courts. In 630 Fursey, later to become the first Bishop of the Anglians, arrived at the court. He, and his successors Follian and Ultán, would have witnessed the Anglian artistry and may even (for the Irish Church is known to have possessed brooches itself) have commissioned work which then found its way back to Ireland, Northumbria and Iona.

The first half of the seventh century also saw the Celtic Church at its most ebullient and confident and some of the major continental foundations, which were finally to number ninety-four, were made during this period. These foundations acted as conduits for the precious manuscripts of the Middle East but the Celtic monks

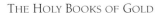
would have come into contact with the Germanic art of the Burgundians, Visigoths and Merovingian Franks, some of whom were Christian, and who practised elaborate cloisonné enamelling, filigree work and refined rectilinear step patterns. The zoomorphic influences on Durrow are not uniquely Germanic; an older culture is visible in the animal art which harks back to Hallstatt.

Whatever the origin of the influences on Durrow, the effects of the manuscript on religious art generally were immense. From the end of the seventh century broad ribbon meanders begin to appear on stone crosses, such as those of Carndonagh and Fahan Mura, and the Ardagh chalice, produced more than a century later, shares with Durrow the use of blank backgrounds to throw design into relief.

After Durrow, the finest scriptoria work passed to Northumberland, to Whitby, Old Melrose, Jarrow, Ripon, Durham and to Lindisfarne itself, the tiny but vital foundation which lay just off the coast of Northumberland, battered by east winds and rough seas, where manuscript production reached its most prolific within the Celtic Church. The monastic community at Lindisfarne had been established in 635 when Oswald, King of Northumbria, invited Columba's successor, Aidan of Iona, to bring the Celtic Church to the court and people of the north-east. Oswald gave him a small, windswept island, close to the rocky headland of Bamburgh but cut off by the tide twice a day. Here Aidan began to build a community along the lines of Iona with cells made of simple oak logs thatched with reeds. Over the next decades, numerous monastic communities were founded, many on or near coastal sites, and the passion for learning that had inspired Iona spread like fire to the north of England.

The royal connection was significant and was to have far-reaching consequences for the Church as a whole. Bede tells us that the Northumbrian court was torn between the Roman and Celtic practices. Oswald, who favoured the Irish Celtic, was killed in battle just two years after Aidan's arrival and his successor Oswy had grown up within the Roman Church of St Augustine. The differences between the two Churches were, on the surface, about the date of Easter and the tonsure. The Celts calculated Easter according to the earliest Roman model, which was an 84-year cycle of repetition of lunar and solar cycles from AD 32, while the Roman Church worked on a reformed 19-year cycle brought into use in 525. The Celtic tonsure was in druidic style, that is they shaved the hair from ear to ear over the top of the head and let it grow long at the back. The Romans, in an imitation of the crown of thorns, shaved a circle on the top of the head. In fact the issues were more complex, revolving around the particular emphases of the international centralized Church (the Roman) and the uncentralized provincial one (the Celtic). The simple ritual and liturgy of the Celtic Church was at odds with the dogma and bureaucracy of the Roman. The Celts had monk-priests, the Romans had bishops. The Celts developed a practice of private confession, while the Romans preferred public. The Celts put nature at the centre of their understanding of God, while the Romans concentrated on God's creation, man, who was, so the gospels said, 'made in his image'.

In 663 the royal court of Northumbria celebrated two Easters at different dates in an attempt to satisfy both churches. Clearly it was an untenable situation and the following year a synod was called to resolve the matter once and for all. At the Synod of Whitby, held in 664, the Celts were represented by Colman and Chad, later to be Bishop of Lichfield; the Romans by Wilfrid, Abbot of Ripon, and a Gaulish bishop. Oswy, swayed by the argument of the foundation of the Christian Church on the rock of Peter, chose Roman Christianity for Northumberland.

Colman, unable to reconcile himself to dominance from Rome returned to Iona at the end of the Whitby Synod. But for all that the Irish were vanquished, their scholarship remained. Lindisfarne assumed the mantle of mature Irish scholarship and the ethos of the Irish approach was maintained. Cuthbert, brought in from Melrose to reform the customs of the Lindisfarne monastery along Roman lines, revealed the ascetic streak of his training and character by retreating as a hermit to Inner Farne, two miles out to sea opposite Bamburgh. His reputation as a holy man spread and when he died on 20 March 687, miracles were subsequently reported at his tomb. When his tomb was opened on the day of his elevation to the altar on 20 March 698, his body was found to be incorrupt, a further proof of his saintliness.

T HE LINDISFARNE GOSPELS, MADE, ACCORDING TO THE COLOPHON added in the mid-tenth century, 'in honour of God and St Cuthbert by Eadfrith, Bishop of Lindisfarne', were probably executed between 687 and 698. Three hundred years later Aldred, 'unworthy and most miserable priest', as he described himself, wrote a colophon or history of the book in Anglo-Saxon and added, in what would be seen today as an extraordinary act of vandalism and egotism, his own translation, word for word, above the Latin text. It is without literary merit, but of great historical interest and is perhaps indicative of how, once the novelty of Christianity had worn off, congregations and monks sought edification in their own language. Words from Aldred's gloss are also included in the first dictionary of the English language, compiled in the late sixteenth century in the reign of Elizabeth I.

Initial letter of Marcus, St Mark's Gospel, folio 90, Lindisfarne Gospels, c. 698. The tenth-century Anglo-Saxon translation written in by Aldred, 'miserable and unworthy priest', is visible above the Latin text. Within the initial letter, two lions, the symbol of St Mark, spew their tongues.
BRITISH LIBRARY

incipit euangelium secundum iohan

IN PRIN
CIPIO
ERAT UERBUM
ET UERBUM ERAT
ABUD DM DX

The majority of the book is undecorated text but there are fifteen pages of full decoration: four images of the evangelists which lie at the front of each gospel, four cross-carpet pages, and four huge initial letters. Of the remaining three decorative pages, there is an additional initial page in Matthew, the magnificent Chi Rho which marks the start of the Christmas gospel, and a carpet page and initial page to introduce St Jerome's letter to Pope Damasus, which explains and elucidates his translation into Latin of the gospel texts.

The Lindisfarne Gospel is a *tour de force* of technical skills. It was here that the art of bird and animal interlace, which was also to recur in the Lichfield Gospels, was perfected on invisible grids of elongated pagan Ss. Animals and birds are a feature of Eadfrith's work and the Lindisfarne Gospels is the first surviving insular manuscript in which birds play a large part in the decoration. It was the Germanic zoomorphic influence at play, but the Celts added their own flourishes. Quite unlike the fantasy birds and beasts of Saxon art, those under the brush and quill of the Lindisfarne monks were depicted in a more naturalistic way. The east coast, and Lindisfarne particularly, was the haunt of sea birds – cormorants and kittiwakes – and nesting eagles, and the Northumbrians, although under the sway of Rome, were reflecting the world around them and decorating their sacred texts with the wonders of God's creation which informed their daily lives.

In this context the images of the evangelists, which show Byzantine and Roman influence in their classical dress and faces, can be compared to other local phenomena, including Roman remains which by now, some four centuries later, had become part of

Initial page of St John's Gospel, folio 211, Lindisfarne Gospels, c. 698. It reads 'In Principio erat verbum' (In the beginning was the word), the main emphasis of the page falling the letters I, N and P. The decoration of the dropped I has been compared to the iron chain of the huge Sutton Hoo cauldron. The only human face to appear in the text of the Lindisfarne Gospels is just visible in the green C of Principio.
BRITISH LIBRARY

the landscape. A comparison has been drawn between the images of the evangelists that appear on the pages of the Lindisfarne Gospels with a stone-carved grave-slab of Romano-British origin found at Murrell Hill near Carlisle, on which a seated, classical figure is attended by a winged genius overhead. If this was the model, it makes sense of the seated evangelists, resplendent in classical dress, and all attended by companion symbols: Matthew, a winged man; Mark a lion; Luke a calf; and John an eagle.

Just as the broad ribbon meanders of Durrow ended up on the crosses of Carndonagh and Fahan Mura and were duplicated in the stone crosses of Ireland, so in Northumberland, too, ideas spread across the decorative arts. Ribbon interlace passed to panels of the eighth-century great stone cross at Bewcastle in Cumbria and inter-locking birds appear in the eighth-centurey stone cross at Aberlay, Lothian.

HERE ARE THREE OTHER BOOKS OF GOSPELS THAT BEAR THE MARK OF THE Lindisfarne scriptorium in one way or another. The Durham Gospels, which survive in fragments, are written in a similar insular majuscule and contain the same Northumbrian Romano-British portraits of evangelists. Carpet and initial pages follow the Lindisfarne model, while a new addition, perhaps due to the influence of Rome now upon the foundation, are scenes from the life of Christ. The Otho-Corpus Gospels, which are now divided between the British Library and Corpus Christi College, Cambridge, show every sign of being created at the Lindisfarne scriptorium. Finally, there are the Echternach Gospels, so-called because they were owned by the abbey of Echternach founded by the Northumbrian St Willibrord in 698.

Of all these the most complete and most interesting are the Echternach Gospels which combine features of the Iona and Northumberland traditions. They were written in insular miniscule for speed, and followed the form of Lindisfarne with full-page

miniatures of the evangelists and initial pages, but are without carpet pages. Since they are written on vellum of continental preparation, it is fair to assume that the monastery sent the goods and perhaps even the colours – red, yellow, purple – to be used at Lindisfarne. The Durham and Echternach Gospels may be the work of a single scribe and artist but there are also differences between the manuscripts and it is possible that the production was done variously by different people and in different places. In its use of initials, the Echternach is very similar to Durham, while effervescent decoration of the Chi-Rho owes something to the hanging-bowl tradition of Durrow.

Willibrord was a Northumbrian and began his religious life at Wilfrid's Ripon. He was a disciple of an abbot called Egbert who preached in the Roman manner amongst the Irish and Scots and brought Romanization to the Pictish Church, persuading the Iona monks in 716 to accept the Roman Easter and eventually to adopt the Roman tonsure. He effectively brought about a unification of Iona with Northumbria which also saw the absorption of the Picts. Willibrord was part of one of Egbert's continental missions and after two years as Archbishop of Utrecht, he founded a monastery at Echternach in 698. This coincided with the elevation of St Cuthbert to the altar at Lindisfarne and since the scriptorium was preparing the Lindisfarne Gospels, they may also have offered to prepare the Echternach Gospels.

The Echternach Gospels contain a number of illuminated pages of particular interest. The symbol of Matthew, with the intention of emphasizing his seraphic nature, looks for all the world like a Victorian choirboy, and there are naturalistic animal symbols of Luke, Mark and John. Matthew has a Roman tonsure, an acknowledgment of the debt of influence that Willibrord owed to Egbert, and the influence Egbert had in the expansion of the Roman Church. The animal evangelist symbols, again acknowledging Egbert and his work in the north of Scotland, are wonderfully Pictish. The eagle is a replica of the Pictish design at Knowe of Burrian, Orkney and dates from the first half of the seventh century. Perhaps the artist himself was Pictish.

T HE PASSIONATE CERTAINTY AND URGE FOR EXPANSION OF THE Celtic Irish Church was affected after the Whitby Synod. Iona continued to be an outstanding model of Celtic monasticism, but elsewhere standards relaxed in the seventh and eighth centuries. Abbeys and monasteries grew richer, and abbacies became hereditary and the preserve of royal families. Abbots, we are told, assumed the habit of kings, even to the extent of fighting pitched battles with other monasteries as they effectively established small kingdoms. As religious practices in the monasteries declined, however, something of the old, ascetic spirit revived. The Culdees or Friends of God formed an association of hermits in the eighth century, living in solitude in the most remote places, and re-applying some of the rigours

For all the world like a Victorian choirboy: the symbol of St Matthew, 'Imagio Hominis', or image of man, from the Echternach Gospels, folio 18, c. 700. Matthew wears a Roman tonsure, shaved on the top of his head, in acknowledgment of the supremacy of the Roman church over the Celtic. Celtic monks shaved their heads from ear to ear and let the hair grow down behind.
BIBLIOTHEQUE NATIONALE, PARIS

IMAGO hominis

of the desert ascetics to their way of life. A religious and artistic renaissance followed as the example of the Culdees chastened the monasteries to reform their religious practices. Once again, the scriptoria began to copy the sacred texts and in this century the manuscript tradition flourished, and the poetry and old tales of the Celts were written down. From this period came the illumination of the great Book of Kells, the high stone crosses and the fabulous church metalwork of the Ardagh and Derryflanan chalices.

The Book of Kells is the largest and most ornate of the manuscripts of the Gospels 33 × 24 cm and is written in round, half-uncial majuscule hand on thick-glazed vellum. It was probably inscribed at Iona in the last years of the eighth century, or the early years of the ninth, the time boundaries being those of Viking raids which shook the island on a number of occasions and which resulted, in 806, in the death of sixty-eight of the community. In 807 the decision was taken to build a new foundation at Kells. According to the Annals of Ulster, this was the 'new monastery of Colum Cille' and it was completed with great speed. The consecration of the new monastery was the force behind the creation of a new, magnificent book of gospels. Alternatively, the manuscript may have been started at Iona and finished at Kells.

No other early Christian manuscript in Western Europe is so lavishly produced and only two of its 680 pages have no colour. It is the most sophisticated expression of manuscript art and represents the high-water mark in the ability of Irish scribes and artists to conceive, plan and execute. They exhibit a freedom of artistic expression and range of imagination which is remarkable, and quite different from that of the formulaic Northumbrian scriptoria. Particularly striking are the incidentals, the animals, birds

Opening Page, or Chi-Rho, of the St Matthew Christmas Gospel, folio 34, Book of Kells, c. 800. The page represents the high-water mark of Celtic manuscript artistry. It is pure La Tène in its swirling, voluptuous spirals and triskeles. The pagan and the Christian, represented by the head of Christ in the letter P, sit comfortably together.
TRINITY COLLEGE, DUBLIN

and figures who appear seemingly in the most casual way, amongst the pages of text. These include a horse and rider, the horseman's foot pointing for emphasis at the phrase 'and on the third day he shall rise again' (*Et tertia die resurget*), two mice fighting over a communion wafer, a Pictish wolf stalking along the lines of Matthew and a lizard basking on a spring day amongst the pages of Mark. Sheep, cats, hounds, hares and moths wander at will over the pages.

Much of the decoration is redolent with Christian symbolism. Christ is portrayed as fish, lion, snake and peacock. The fish, used as the symbol of Christ is the salmon, which also appears on the escutcheons from hanging bowls from Sutton Hoo. The snake, in the shedding of its skin, signifies Christ's resurrection, as does the lion because, according to a Greek legend, lion cubs are born dead but are revived by their father's breathing on the third day. The peacock represents the incorruptibility of Christ, because peacock flesh, according to classical legend, does not rot.

The historian Françoise Henry has detected the hand of three major artists and four scribes in the manuscript. The first artist she calls 'the Goldsmith', for his use of yellow and silvery blue colour, but also for the relationship between his work and the metalwork of the time. He may, of course, have been a metalworker as well as a manuscript artist. To him, Mlle Henry attributes the dazzling eight-circle cross, the Chi-Rho of the Christmas gospels and the Initium of St Mark. She dubs the second artist 'the Illustrator' for his narrative depictions of the Temptation, the arrest of Christ, and the Virgin and Child. Her third man, responsible for the images of Christ, St Matthew and St John, is 'the portrait painter'.

Eight-Circle Cross at the start of St Matthew's Gospel, folio 33, Book of Kells, c. 800. Françoise Henry believed the page to be the work of the artist she calls the Goldsmith, because of the parallels between this and metalwork of the time. The delicacy of the roundels mimics the filigree and niello work of the Tara Brooch.
TRINITY COLLEGE, DUBLIN

In 1185 a man called Giraldus Cambrensis saw the Book of Kells at Kildare and wrote the following description:

> It contains the concordance of the four gospels according to Saint Jerome, with almost as many drawings as pages, and all of them in marvellous colours. Here you can look upon the face of the divine majesty drawn in a miraculous way; here too upon the mystical representations of the Evangelists now having six, now four, and now two, wings. Here you will see the eagle; there the calf. Here the face of a man; there that of a lion . . . If you look at them carelessly and casually and not too closely, you may judge them to be mere daubs rather than careful compositions. You will see nothing subtle where everything is subtle. But if you take the trouble to look very closely, and penetrate with your eyes to the secrets of the artistry, you will notice such intricacies, so delicate and subtle, so close together, and well-knitted, so involved and bound together, and so fresh still in their colourings that you will not hesitate to declare that all these things must have been the result of the work, not of men, but of angels.

Kells, the highpoint of the manuscript tradition of the Celtic Church, was complemented by one final masterpiece. The Ardagh chalice is the most famous piece of early Irish Christian metalwork, and would have been a valued and famous treasure of a monastic community. While its form is simple – it is a large two-handled cup of beaten silver on a silver stem – it is decorated in the most refined and beautiful way.

Ardagh chalice, the most famous piece of early Irish Christian metalwork, mid eighth century. This two-handled cup of beaten silver, marks the transition of Celtic artistry from the Iron and Dark Ages into a highly developed aesthetic art of the Medieval period.
TRINITY COLLEGE, DUBLIN

THE CELTIC LEGACY

ONA FLOURISHED AGAIN AS A HOLY PLACE AFTER THE VIKING RAIDS. THE monastery was rebuilt and by the eleventh century was part of a new Norse diocese which included the Hebrides and the Isle of Man. Its sanctity made it the burial place of Scottish, Irish and Norwegian kings throughout the medieval period. The Celtic Church in Ireland maintained its independence until the twelfth century, when it finally relinquished its tonsure and adherence to the old dates of Easter, and was absorbed into the Roman Church. Columbanus's love of devotional solitude and talking to the birds and the bees, a gloriously Celtic preoccupation if ever there was one, was revived at its ascetic root by a single man in the

The Arrest of Christ, St Matthew's Gospel, folio 144, Book of Kells, c. 800. Scenes from the life of Christ are a feature of Kells and would have been copied from continental manuscripts. Christ's divinity is symbolized by his blond hair. In battle, the Celts wore their hair bleached and thickened with powdered lime which gave them a fair appearance. The garden of Gethsemane, above Christ's head, is illustrated with the Pictish tree of life symbols.
TRINITY COLLEGE, DUBLIN

83

Roman Church in the thirteenth century: Francis or Francesco of Assisi, who took the creed of Columbanus as the basis for his monastic foundation.

Despite Christianity, the old beliefs died hard. Two stories, both with supernatural elements, grew around the Books of Lindisfarne and Kells. The first concerned the loss overboard, as if in imitation of the old votive offerings, of the Lindisfarne Gospels on the journey between Lindisfarne and the mainland in the ninth century. The second concerned the theft of the Book of Kells from the monastery at Kells. Both were found intact, the former as a result of a holy vision, the second 'after two months and twenty nights', during which it lay, consigned to the safety of Mother Earth, 'covered by a sod'.

The great Celtic festivals also marched sturdily into medieval life. *Samhain* (31 October/1 November) is the Celtic new year, the boundary between summer and winter, when time and space are frozen, the Otherworld being so close that its spirits walk on earth and humans may freely enter and return from its domains. *Beltane*, or the festival of Bright or Goodly Fire (1 May), encourages, by the driving of cattle between bonfires, fertility, purification and the warmth of the earth. *Lughnasad* (1 August) celebrates and protects the harvest, and *Imbolc* (1 February) encourages the lactation of ewes. They survived because, like Celtic art itself, they represented ways of seeing which were underpinned by the seasons of the year and the vagaries of the natural world.

One of the more surprising aspects of the Celtic legacy are the eighty or so carvings of female genitalia that appear on churches in Ireland. Little to do with Christianity, except perhaps as a warning against excessive lust, they express the far older heritage of rightful kingship in Ireland, the mating of kings with the fertility goddess, which was never exorcised from the Irish Celtic consciousness. Gargoyles, found a-plenty on churches throughout the British Isles, perform a similar function. These strange, contorted faces, now leering, now melancholic beyond comfort, are the direct descendants of the Celtic severed head, that battle trophy and supernatural mask that occurs and recurs in the Iron Age culture.

Most delightful of all is the rich vein of legends and romances the Celts left behind. The concept of courtly love, which played so intrinsic a part in the medieval literary

tradition, was Arabic in origin and passed, with the spread of Islam in the tenth century, first to Spain and then into France where it became the preserve and *métier* of the troubadours. However, the Celtic love of poets and their narrative tales was older and indigenously European. The love stories of Tristan and Iseult, Grainne and Diarmaid, Lancelot and Guinevere, the elegiac tale of Deirdre and the Sons of Usna, all have their roots in the great Celtic bardic tradition that sprang from a people carrying their history with them for handing down from generation to generation.

The Celts survive to this day. The Irish, Scots, Welsh, Manx, Cornish and Bretons are the guardians of the Celtic languages and oral traditions. Storytellers, songsters, adventurers still, Irish men and women set forth from their homeland to live, travel and establish communities abroad more than any other European people. They maintain a great heritage whose contribution to European culture, art and society is as vital and energetic as ever.

A Celtic Chronology

CELTIC ARTWORKS
Early Irish goldwork from 1,400 BC
Gold openwork bowl from Schwazenbrach
5th C BC
Bronze flagon from Lorraine 4th C BC
Witham shield 2nd C BC
Battersea shield 1st C BC
Snettisham torque 1st C BC
Battersea shield 1st C BC

Bronze figurine of Celtic Smith God from
Sunderland AD 2–3 C
Sceptre mounted by bronze stag from
Sutton Hoo AD 634
Hinged shoulder clasp from Sutton Hoo
AD 634
Fuller fibula AD 7th C
Tara brooch AD 8th C

Book of Durrow 680
Lindisfarne Gospels 698
Echtenach Gospels 700
Lichfield Gospels 720
Ardagh chalice mid-8th C
Book of Kells 800

CELTIC CULTURE
Bronze Age 2,400–700 BC
Iron Age 700 BC–AD 300
Hallstatt (Europe only) 700 BC–400 BC

La Tène (Europe and Britain and Ireland)
500 BC–1st C AD
Roman metalworking techniques introduced to
Britain 1st–2nd C
Manuscript art of the monastic scriptoria
650–825

CELTIC HISTORY
Celts begin to settle in Britain and Ireland
2,400 BC
Continental Celts at height of power 400–270 BC
Celts sack Rome 397 BC
Celts sack Delphi 270 BC
Celts pushed back to central Europe 225 BC
Caesar invades Gaul and makes foray to Britain
64–52 BC
Romans invade Britain AD 43
Boudica defeated by Romans AD 60
Completion of Hadrian's Wall AD 123
Christianity reaches Britain 2nd–3rd C
St Ninian builds a church in Galloway, Candida
Casa AD 400
The coming of Patrick to Ireland AD 432
Roman withdrawal from Britain and Saxon
advance AD 410
Battle of Badon AD 493
Columba establishes a monastery on Iona
AD 563
St Aidan establishes a monastery on Lindisfarne
AD 635
Synod of Whitby AD 664

GLOSSARY

ANIMAL INTERLACE
Design of the interlocked stylized animals and beasts which originated in Germanic art of the fourth and fifth centuries. Animal and bird interlace was a feature of manuscript illumination, particularly in the Lindisfarne Gospels.

ANNULAR BROOCHES
Brooches in the shape of a ring, popular in Scotland and Ireland following the Roman occupation.

BOSSES
Domed central part of the shield which conceals and protects the handgrip.

CHALICE
Large ornamental cup for the blessing and distribution of the Eucharist wine.

CHAMPLEVÉ ENAMEL
Technique whereby molten or powdered glass is applied to a sunken surface for decorational effect. It originated in La Tène, but became a speciality of British insular art, appearing first on shields and subsequently on jewellery.

CHI-RHO
Name used for the opening initial pages of St Matthew's Christmas Gospel. The letters X, P, I are the abbreviation of the Greek XPI TO.

CIRE-PERDU
Lost-wax process (qv).

CLOISONNÉ ENAMEL
Method of decoration involving enamel set in individual and delicate gold cells, and typical of the jewellery of Sutton Hoo.

COMMAS
Trumpet or comma shapes, often referred to as trumpet or comma voids because, in insular art, the shapes were frequently left undecorated.

CURVILINEAR
Composed in curved lines - typical of Celtic art from La Tène.

DRAGON/LYRE PAIRS
Dragon shapes put on the lyre S-shaped grid, so they faced each other in pairs. Both dragons and lyres were motifs with Eastern origins.

FILIGREE
Fine wires of gold or silver which were used to outline designs on jewellery and metalwork. It was a technique initially borrowed from the Romans.

LOST-WAX PROCESS
Metal casting process in which an object is first moulded in wax. Soft clay is pressed around it which is then baked so that the wax is released. The clay is then used as a mould into which metal can be poured.

LYRES
Greek motif in which two mirrored S-shapes face one another. It was a favourite device for decorating shields and swords in the La Tène period.

LYRE-PALMETTES
Two mirrored S-shapes have the space between the Ss at the top filled with a downwards palmette design. It was used for decorating shields and swords in the La Tène period.

MILLEFIORI
Roman decorative technique involving bundles of rods of coloured glass, heated to fusion point and then sliced across to provide inserts for jewellery and trinkets. Another technique was to twist different coloured rods together and slice them off, which produced a multicoloured swirling effect.

NIELLO
Black compound of silver or copper sulphide, inlaid for decorative contrast in jewellery from the sixth century.

OPENWORK GOLDWEAR
Fine goldwork which has a fretwork appearance, often composed in a design of leaf motifs and found as a decoration for the top of drinking horns and drinking cups in La Tène barrow graves.

PALMETTES
Classical Greek motif of palm leaves, often used in association with lotus buds. The Celts transformed it into an abstract motif, which occurs regularly through the La Tène period. Half-palmettes, that is the left or right side of the design, were continued on into S-shaped curves, and appear on the Witham shield of the second century BC.

PATEN
Church dish used to hold the bread or wafers for Communion.

PENANNULAR
In the shape of a ring, with a small gap in the circle. Brooches like this became part of the Celtic repertoire after the Roman departure.

REPOUSSÉ
Raised designs, particularly found on Iron Age shields, created by hammering shapes into the back of the shield.

SNAIL-SHELL SPIRALS
Designs of spiral circles, resembling shells, which were a feature of La Tène. They also appear in the Chi-Rho pages of the insular gospels.

STEP PATTERNS
Geometric patterns absorbed from Germanic and continental art in the seventh and eighth centuries. They are a feature of the carpet pages of the Lindisfarne Gospels.

TENDRILS
Lines which curl and run off main designs as decorative features. The Greek wave tendril was a running frieze of triangles where the three points of each triangle were continued into a curled spiral.

TRISKELE
Circular design where three curves radiate from a central point. A Celtic design, it is preserved in the three-legged motif of the Isle of Man.

ZOOMORPHIC
Designs in the form of animals or parts of animals.

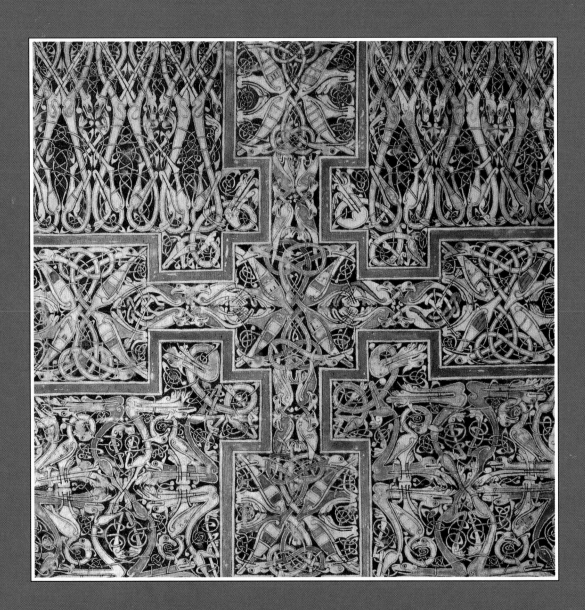